25 WAL

IN THE
SOUTH
PENNINES

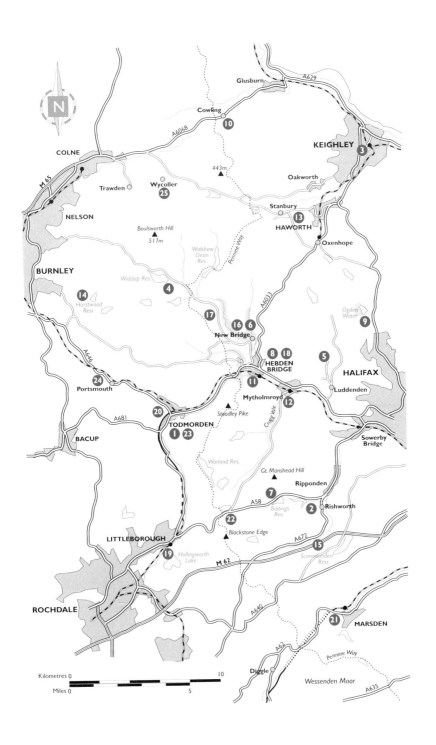

25 WALKS

IN THE

SOUTH PENNINES

John Manning

Series Editor: Roger Smith

EDINBURGH: THE STATIONERY OFFICE

Applications for reproduction should be made to The Stationery Office Ltd,
South Gyle Crescent, Edinburgh EH12 9EB

Acknowledgements

While compiling this book I've been more than grateful for the tolerant
company and advice of many friends and family members, including Liz,
Matthew and Rebecca Watkins, David and Caroline Manning, Helen
Manning, Caroline Brearley, Helena Smith, Phil Smith, Andrew Harrison
and Michael Denton. I'd also like to thank Mick Chatham and David
Nortcliffe, of Calderdale Countryside Service, Tony Philpin of the Pennine
Way Co-ordination Project, as well as my parents, Peter and Barbara
Manning, for allowing me to temporarily return to the nest while researching
the walks. Special thanks are due to the book's editor, Roger Smith, for his
patience and encouragement.

Photographs: John Manning
Photographs: Walks 2, 7 and 22: Paul Hannon

British Library Cataloguing in Publication Data

A catalogue record for this book is available from the British Library

ISBN 0 11 495824 6

CONTENTS

USEFUL INFORMATION

The length of each walk is given in kilometres and miles, but within the text measurements are metric for simplicity. The walks are described in detail and are supported by accompanying maps (study them before you start the walk), so there is little likelihood of getting lost. However, on some of the moorland walks you would be wise to carry a compass and a copy of the Ordnance Survey South Pennines 1:25 000 Outdoor Leisure map, which is widely available in the area and covers all the walks in the book with the exception of Walk 21, Marsden Moor, which crosses on to the Peak District – Dark Peak Outdoor Leisure sheet.

Every care has been taken to make the descriptions and maps as accurate as possible, but the author and publishers can accept no responsibility for errors, however caused. The countryside is always changing and there will inevitably be alterations to some aspects of these walks as time goes by. The publishers and author would be happy to receive comments and suggested alterations for future editions of the book.

Tourist Information Centres

Town Hall, Bow Street, Keighley BD21 3PA. Tel: 01535 618014. Fax: 01535 690807.
The Piece Hall, Halifax HX1 1RE. Tel: 01422 368725. Fax: 01422 354264.
1 Bridge Gate, Hebden Bridge HX7 8EX. Tel: 01422 843831. Fax: 01422 845266.
15 Burnley Road, Todmorden OL14 7BU. Tel & Fax: 01706 818181.
2-4 West Lane, Haworth BD22 8EF. Tel: 01535 642329. Fax: 01535 647721.
49-51 Huddersfield Road, Holmfirth HD7 1JP. Tel: 01484 222444. Fax: 01484 222445.

Countryside Centres

Bracken Hall Countryside Centre, Glen Road, Baildon, Shipley, Bradford BD17 5EA. Tel: 01274 584140.
Healey Dell Nature Reserve Visitor Centre, Healey

METRIC MEASUREMENTS

At the beginning of each walk, the distance is given in miles and kilometres. Within the text, all measurements are metric for simplicity (and indeed our Ordnance Survey maps are now all metric). However, it was felt that a conversion table might be useful to those readers who still tend to think in terms of miles.

The basic statistic to remember is that one kilometre is five-eighths of a mile. Half a mile is equivalent to 800 metres and a quarter-mile is 400 metres. Below that distance, yards and metres are little different in practical terms.

km	miles
1	0.625
1.6	1
2	1.25
3	1.875
3.2	2
4	2.5
4.8	3
5	3.125
6	3.75
6.4	4
7	4.375
8	5
9	5.625
10	6.25
16	10

Hall Mills, Dell Road, Shawclough, Rochdale OL12 6BG. Tel & fax: 01706 378481.

Hollingworth Lake Country Park Visitor Centre, Rakewood Road, Littleborough OL15 0AQ. Tel: 01706 373421. Fax: 01706 378753.

Oakwell Hall Country Park, Nutter Lane, Birstall WF17 9LG. Tel: 01924 326240. Fax: 01924 326249.

Ogden Water Countryside Centre, Ogden Lane, Halifax HX2 8YA. Tel: 01422 249136.

Tunnel End Canal and Countryside Centre, Waters Road, Marsden HD7 6NQ. Tel: 01484 846062. Fax: 01484 841554.

Wycoller Country Park, The Aisled Barn, Wycoller, Trawden BB8 8SY. Tel & fax: 01282 870253.

Public Transport Information
West Yorkshire: Metroline, 0113 245 7676.
Greater Manchester: GMPTE, 0161 228 7811.
Lancashire: The Bus Station, 01772 556618.
Keighley and Worth Valley Railway, 01535 647777 (24 hours) or 01535 645214.
TransPennine Express: 01482 326033 or 0113 244 8133.

Countryside Services
Bradford Countryside Service, 8th Floor, Jacobs Well, Bradford BD1 5RW. Tel: 01274 752666. Fax: 01274 753767.

Burnley Rights of Way Officer, Burnley Borough Council, PO Box 29, Burnley BB11 2DT. Tel: 01282 425011 ext 2542.

Calderdale Countryside Service, Leisure Services Department, Wellesley Park, Halifax HX2 0AY. Tel: 01422 359454. Fax: 01422 342499.

Kirklees Countryside Unit, The Stables, Ravensknowle Park, Wakefield Road, Huddersfield HD5 8DJ. Tel: 01484 223806.

Lancashire Countryside Service, Planning Department, PO Box 160, East Cliff County Offices, Preston PR1 3EX. Tel: 01772 264709. Fax: 01772 264201.

National Trust, Hardcastle Crags, Hollin Hall Estate Office, Crimsworth Dean, Hebden Bridge, West Yorkshire HX7 7AP. Tel & fax: 01422 844518.

National Trust, Marsden Moor Estate Office, The Old Goods Yard, Station Road, Marsden, Huddersfield HD7 6DH. Tel: 01484 847016. Fax: 01484 847071.

North West Water Conservation, Access and Recreation Officer, Rivington Water Treatment Works, Bolton Road, Horwich BL8 7RN. Tel 01204 696118. Fax: 01204 669237.

Rochdale Countryside Service, Visitor Centre, Hollingworth Lake Country Park, Rakewood Road, Littleborough OL15 0AQ. Tel: 01706 373421. Fax: 01706 378753.

INTRODUCTION

The Pennine Chain, which rises along the centre of northern England like a spine from the Midlands north to the Tyne Gap, holds special treasures for hillwalkers: the Peak District National Park, the Yorkshire Dales National Park, and the North Pennines Area of Outstanding Natural Beauty are well known to those who enjoy exploring wild places on foot. The South Pennines, however, could justifiably be called the forgotten vertebrae on the backbone of England.

When, in the 1940s, the Hobhouse Committee examined the suitability of various areas for designation as National Parks, the South Pennines was somehow overlooked. Today, while crowds of walkers, tourists and holidaymakers flock to the neighbouring National Parks, the South Pennines' beautiful expanses of wild moors and wooded cloughs offer peace and solitude.

Defining the area is no easy task – the South Pennines is not strictly speaking a geographical region, but more an attempt by several local authorities working together to promote the area for recreation and tourism. Straddling the Yorkshire/Lancashire boundary between the Peak District and the Yorkshire Dales, it offers tremendously varied walking along ancient causey paths, packhorse routes, towpaths and bridleways, through a landscape pockmarked with the relics of a rich industrial past.

Away from the valley bottom towns such as Hebden Bridge, Todmorden and Marsden, whose mills thrived during the Industrial Revolution, you can find the crumbling skeletal ruins of earlier, water-powered mills, their chimneys poking above the tree canopies in peaceful cloughs.

This is a landscape which has inspired some of our greatest literary names – the Brontë sisters of Haworth, Poet Laureate Ted Hughes of Mytholmroyd, Halifax-born Phyllis Bentley and Bradford's J. B. Priestley all drew inspiration from the environment in which they were raised. The source of that inspiration can only be sensed; it is in the romance of the moors, the charm of the valleys, the rugged friendliness of the inhabitants and even in the wind-worn Millstone Grit that predominates in the area, and which influenced sculptor Henry Moore's famous works. The stone, used to build the drystone walls, houses and mills, is most evident in the hills where long ridges of the coarse sandstone tear their way from the very earth. Many of the 17th and 18th century stone farmhouses and weavers' cottages, with their mullioned windows and blackened walls, seem almost to have grown from the ground.

The rock was laid down by a vast river delta which covered the country 280 million years ago. Earth movements, glaciers and the elements shaped the rock over the centuries, creating the rounded hills and deep valleys we can still see today. Much of the area would once have been blanketed by forest –

in deep upland peat you will occasionally find the bleached root-balls of birch or Scots pine trees, preserved for thousands of years – but man's need for timber and grazing land saw the forests felled. Constant nibbling by livestock meant the woods never regenerated and instead the moorland vegetation – heather, bilberry, cotton grass and carpets of coarse grasses – took hold on the peaty soils.

But this is no barren landscape. The boggy upland environment provides a habitat for a rich diversity of birdlife, from waders such as the curlew, the golden plover and the dunlin, to game birds such as the red grouse and partridge, and birds of prey including the spectacular merlin and ghostly short-eared owl. Large tracts of moorland have recently been protected under European law because of their importance for ground nesting birds. The cloughs which drain those moors are home to fly-catcher, green woodpecker, grey wagtail, dipper, kingfisher and heron. In those woodlands you might be lucky enough to see roe deer, catch a fleeting glimpse of a red squirrel or spot signs of badger, fox or stoat.

The walks in this book vary from 3 km to 17 km (2-11 miles) and many are suitable for families. Those with younger children should bear in mind, however, that an open moor in deteriorating weather might not be the best place to get youngsters acquainted with the great outdoors! Shorter, low level walks, such as Luddenden Dean and Ryburn Reservoir, provide excellent introductions to the delights of walking which shouldn't wear out young feet too quickly. Those with experience will enjoy the longer excursions, such as the ascent of Lad Law, the highest hill in the area, and the classic traverse of Marsden Moor.

The weather is an important consideration. Accurate forecasts can be difficult to obtain as the Pennine hills exert their own influence and conditions can change rapidly; waterproofs are obligatory on most walks, as is good footwear, preferably walking boots. I would strongly advise that you carry a map and compass – and know how to use them – when the weather is poor.

These walks will enable you to sample the best that the South Pennines have to offer and will, I hope, encourage you to explore the area more fully, perhaps along one of the many waymarked paths you will encounter – such as the Rochdale Pioneers Round, the Calderdale Way, the Todmorden Centenary Way and the Colne Valley Circular Walk. In the text you will come across a few local terms which might be unfamiliar: a *clough* is a small tributary valley cut by a stream; a *snicket* is a short, narrow path, usually walled or between hedges; and a *goit* is a man-made water channel, often carrying water to, or from, a mill.

I sincerely hope that you will enjoy your walks around the South Pennines and return to enjoy this magical area many times.

JOHN MANNING

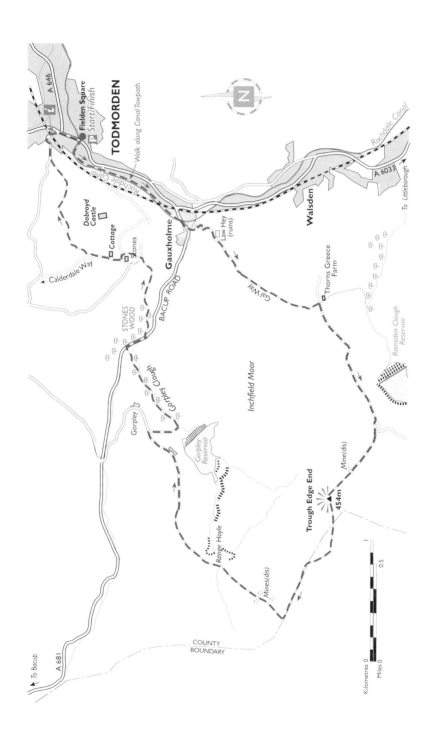

TODMORDEN

Fielden Square
Start/Finish

Walk along Canal Towpath

Rochdale Canal

A 646

A 6033

To Littleborough

Dobroyd
Castle

Cottage

Stones

Calderdale Way

Gauxholme

Law Hey
(ruins)

Walsden

Thorns Greece
Farm

STONES
WOOD

BACUP ROAD

Gal Way

Ramsden Clough
Reservoir

Inchfield Moor

Gorpley Clough

Gorpley

Gorpley
Reservoir

Mine(dis)

Trough Edge End

454m

Range Hoyle

Mines(dis)

To Bacup

A 681

COUNTY
BOUNDARY

Kilometres 0

Miles 0

0.5

GORPLEY RESERVOIR AND STONES

One of the delights of walking the South Pennines is the knowledge that you can climb away from the urban valley environment and be alone on the wind-swept moors within minutes. Though you might escape the 20th century bustle, signs of man's presence are inescapable; ancient packhorse routes, signs of long abandoned mining, weavers' cottages and moorland farms add a particular fascination to the landscape that you'll find nowhere else in the country.

From Fielden Square, join the Rochdale Canal towpath at Todmorden Lock in Rochdale Road

Milepost on the towpath, Todmorden.

and follow the towpath for 1.5km, past Wadsworth Mill Lock and Shade Lock, and under the impressive castellated railway bridge at Gauxholme. At Gauxholme Top Lock, cross the canal and head up Bacup Road for 75m to turn left into Naze Road. By the old tripe works pass through a metal gate at the foot of the old packhorse route and head up the steep zigzag path beyond. Tripe - the lining of a cow or bullock's stomach - has long been a local delicacy, and is usually stewed in milk and served with onions.

By the ruins of Law Hey, which straddle the path, you can look back on Todmorden, where the Town Hall stands like a classical temple among the town's blackened mills. Near the top Naze Road becomes a walled path with wicket gates at either end, from which you emerge on to the edge of Inchfield Moor.

INFORMATION

Distance: 15 km (9.5 miles).

Start and finish: Fielden Square in Rochdale Road, Todmorden. There is a small car park in front of the Golden Lion pub in the square.

Terrain: Extremely varied, from paved packhorse routes and wooded cloughs to open moorland. Boots and waterproofs essential.

Public transport: Todmorden is well served by trains and buses from Halifax, Rochdale and Burnley.

Refreshments: None on route; cafes, restaurants and pubs in Todmorden.

Opening Times: Losang Dragpa offers introductory meditation sessions and vegetarian meals on Fridays nights. Contact Losang Dragpa Centre, Dobroyd Castle, Pexwood Road, Todmorden OL14 7JJ (01706 812247).

The preserved packhorse route across Inchfield Moor.

Turn left on the track ahead for 20m, then bear right, on to the stone-flagged path across the moor, part of the ancient Long Causeway packhorse route between Rochdale and Burnley. This stretch was known as Gal Way after the Galloway ponies, a hardy breed favoured by the men who transported goods throughout the Pennines.

The path meets a track by a small pond, in front of Thorns Greece Farm. Turn right on the track, which snakes across the moor above Ramsden Clough Reservoir. Just beyond the ruins of a farm the track forks: head right and follow Todmorden Centenary Way markers to a stile and, along the track beyond, through the ruins of a 19th century coal mine. Leave the Way briefly here and follow the faint path up the hill ahead, right of a spoil heap, to the trig pillar on Trough Edge End, at 454m the highest point on the Centenary Way, a splendid 32km route opened in May 1996 to commemorate the formation of Todmorden Borough Council on 22 August 1896.

From the summit trig pillar, turn left along the fence to cross a stile, then left again and over a second stile. From that, head away from the wall, across to the wall opposite. Turn right along that, through a metal gate and past a fingerpost, to a ladder stile. Don't climb it; instead turn right, following marker posts down the moor to cross a track.

Follow the intermittently-posted path, signed for Gorpley Reservoir, down the moor. This area is pitted with shafts, pre-1900s remnants of mines which exploited the coal seams beneath your feet. Some are dangerous and it is important to keep clear of fenced areas. The path crosses a clough at Range Hoyle, then follows the left side of a wall to a track; where this forks, 500m after crossing a wooden step stile, go right, down to the cottages near the dam wall. The track goes through a gate, past the cottage and left, past a barn. Follow the track until your feet meet tarmac. There turn right, past reservoir service buildings, to enter Gorpley Clough through a metal gate in the green fence on your left. This wooded ravine, alive with ferns, wood anenome and small waterfalls, was long overgrown and difficult to follow until a Manpower Services team created a delightful short nature trail.

At its foot you turn right, down Bacup Road for 100m, to cross and take the first path on the left, through Stones Wood. At the top of the wood, through a kissing gate, the path crosses fields to a lane by a ruined cottage; bear left to the end of the lane, then left again towards a TV mast, swinging round across the field to a gate in the top left corner, by a small gritstone outcrop. Through the gate turn

left along the tarmac for a few metres to Stones. Turn right past Stones, then follow the Calderdale Way, behind the stable blocks of nearby Dobroyd Castle, a blackened castellated structure built by John Fielden in the 1860s. According to legend he had fallen for a local mill girl but she refused to marry him unless he built a castle for them to live in. The castle is today known as the Losang Dragpa Centre, a Buddhist retreat.

Just past a cottage adorned with stone 'Celtic' heads, climb the stile and walk 50m ahead to the next, over the wall on the right, to follow a field path along the fence to a gate; turn right along the wall

Waterfall in Gorpley Clough.

for 200m to a gate on the right, by a sheep pen. Through that, descend the wallside path to a stile in the bottom right-hand corner. An obvious path beyond leads down, through a small beech wood, to Doghouse Lane. Turn right to return to Todmorden town centre.

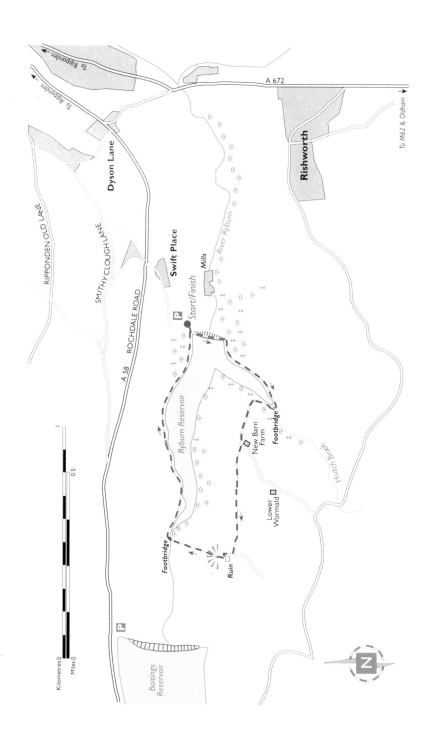

RYBURN RESERVOIR

The damming of the River Ryburn, to create the 10 ha Ryburn Reservoir, was completed between 1925 and 1933 to meet the needs of the population and industry of Wakefield. As with many moorland reservoirs, some ingenious and breathtaking ideas were employed during construction; in this case an aerial ropeway more than 300 m long carried materials from Swift Place, passed on the track down to the car park, to the construction site. Its curved dam wall, 30 m high, holds back nearly 1000 million litres of water.

In the early 1990s, Yorkshire Water and Calderdale Countryside Service created a short stretch of permissive path along the northern shoreline, enabling walkers to enjoy a short but beautiful circular stroll around this picturesque body of water. The walk is particularly rewarding in the autumn, when the contrasting greens and golden browns of the surrounding mixed woodland provide an impressive display of seasonal colour.

Walkers are not alone in enjoying the reservoir area; anglers occasionally try out their fly-fishing skills here and sub-aqua club members have been known to explore the reservoir's 30 m depths.

The track across the curved dam wall gives you a splendid view over the reservoir and the Ryburn Valley as it carries you from the car park to a sound,

INFORMATION

Distance: 3 km (2 miles).

Start and finish: Ryburn Reservoir car park, off George Lane, can be hard to find. Driving west from Ripponden along the A58 Rochdale Road, it is 1.5km out, opposite Nursery Lane and Smithy Clough Lane.

Terrain: Easy field and water-side paths.

Public transport: Buses from Halifax, Littleborough and Rochdale.

Refreshments: Ripponden has a cafe and pubs including the ancient Bridge Inn, by the town's 16th century packhorse bridge.

Note: Because this walk passes through fields use for grazing and because of the birdlife around the reservoir, dogs should be kept on leads at all times.

Tree-fringed Ryburn Reservoir.

made-up path on the opposite bank. Turning right at the far end, past a patch of mixed woodland on your left, cross the first footbridge on your right, beneath which Hutch Brook flows from the peaty uplands of Rishworth Moor into the reservoir.

The trees around this part of the dam provide a roosting area for herons, which you might also sometimes see standing patiently in the shallow edges of the reservoir, waiting to spear small fish or frogs with their long beaks. Bear right, through a narrow strip of trees and over a stile, which thoughtfully incorporates a small gate for dogs.

Over the stile, climb the field ahead, with the wall on your right, into a walled lane which leads towards New Barn Farm. The path heads around the farm on its right side: go through the gate at the top of the field and the waymarked wicket gate ahead. The fenced path beyond leads to a gate and a stile. Having bypassed the farm, the path carries you across two fields, by stiles, to reach another walled lane. Follow this for only a few metres; on the right you'll find a wicket gate, through which a path takes you downhill a short way to the ruins of a farm, from which you have a good view across the upper Ryburn Valley of Manshead End, the summit of Great Manshead Hill.

This area of moorland edge and woodland can rightly be classed as peregrine country. The peregrine falcon is one of Britain's most spectacular birds of prey and the South Pennines has been at the heart of the bird's revival, following persecution, egg theft and the effects of pesticides earlier this century. A protection scheme run by the Royal Society for the Protection of Birds at nearby Booth Wood Reservoir has helped the population recover to what are probably the healthiest numbers since the last war, and the woodlands and rough pasture in the Ryburn Valley provide the bird with excellent hunting territory; the peregrine flies high in the sky until its keen eyes have located its prey. It then plunges in a 'stoop', at speeds of more than 160 km/h (100 mph), and plucks the unfortunate victim from the air.

A wooden fingerpost in front of the decaying building indicates the point at which you head downhill, alongside a wall on your left, to a stile. Over this steps lead down to a footbridge over the ruddy waters of the River Ryburn.

On your left is the huge wall of Baitings Reservoir, built after Ryburn between 1948 and 1956. The wall is more than 500 m wide and holds back 3000 million litres of water, again all originally intended to supply the Wakefield area. A tunnel from Cragg Vale, which runs beneath Manshead Hill, can top up the dam with an extra 15 million litres a day.

From the footbridge the new permissive path, easy to follow on the ground, runs along the water's edge and through woodland, back to the parking area. During the summer Canada geese raise their young on the reservoir, and you'll sometimes find them resting in the grassy picnic areas through which you pass just before the car park.

Looking back across the Ryburn valley.

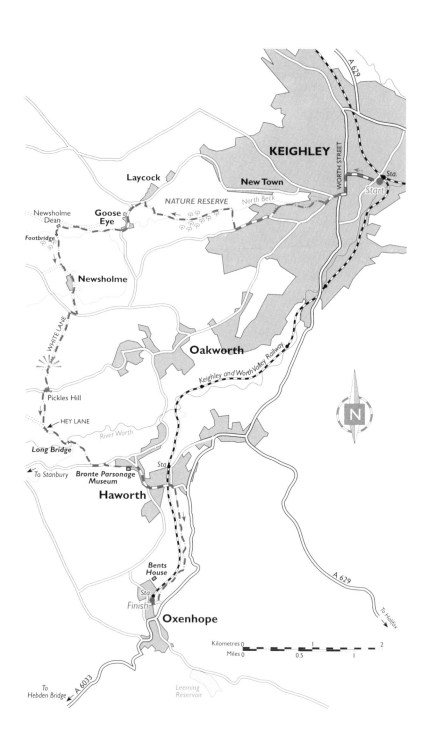

GOOSE EYE AND THE WORTH VALLEY

Not all walks need a theme. Some are simply a delight to follow and this route takes in many wonderful aspects of the South Pennine landscape while managing to avoid the moors, making it an ideal leg-stretch for families or those unsure of their map-reading skills. There are plenty of points of interest along the way, from beautiful stone cottages, ancient packhorse bridges and enchanting wooded cloughs to the fleshpots of Haworth and the excitement of a steam train ride at the end.

Before leaving Keighley Railway Station pick up a timetable for the Worth Valley line; if you linger too long in the Turkey Inn, or in Haworth, you need to be aware of the train times so that you can cut the walk short in Haworth.

From Keighley station head up Cavendish Street and at the top turn left, along Worth Street to the roundabout. Head up Oakworth Road and just past the Royal Mail Delivery Office turn right then immediately left, across North Beck. Follow the landscaped path beyond to head up Becks Road, past Crofton Yarns' mill where the track bears left, following the stream past a ruined mill which straddles the stream.

The two ancient bridges in Newsholme Dean.

INFORMATION

Distance: 15km (9.5 miles) linear.

Start: Keighley Railway Station. Several car parks nearby.

Finish: Oxenhope Railway Station.

Terrain: Wooded cloughs, old lanes and field paths – expect some mud. Boots recommended.

Public transport: Keighley is well served by buses and trains. At weekends and during holiday periods, steam and vintage diesel trains run between Oxenhope and Keighley - highly recommended as a way of rounding off the walk. Timetable details from 01535 645212 or 01535 647777. Buses to Keighley leave Oxenhope every half-hour.

Refreshments: Cafe at Keighley Railway Station; tearooms, pubs and restaurants in Haworth; even a buffet carriage serving hand-pumped ales on the Keighley and Worth Valley Railway. The Turkey Inn at Goose Eye serves meals and has a fine reputation for real ales.

Continued on next page.

Opening hours: The Keighley and Worth Valley Railway runs an excellent free museum at Oxenhope Station, open when trains are running.

East Riddlesden Hall (National Trust) is a merchant's house dating from the time of th English Civil War. Open end Mar-end Oct, Sat-Wed plus Thur in Jul-Aug. Sat 1300-1700; Sun 1100-1700; Mon-Wed (or Thur) 1200-1700. Admission charge (NT members free).

Notes: Stiles and gates between Pickles Hill and Long Bridge were due to be revised at the time of writing and some changes might take place on the ground, although the line of the route will remain the same.

Those arriving in Haworth and wanting to indulge in Brontëdom can cut the walk short by turning left instead of right at the bottom of Bridgehouse Lane to the station, for a steam train ride back to Keighley.

The track carries you up to Fell Lane along which you turn right, past the Three Horses pub. In a further 100m, a signed path on the right takes you back down to the beck and across a footbridge. Turn left and follow the path upstream through lush Holme House Wood, its floor rich with anenome, bluebells, bistort and butterburr. By a second footbridge, not crossed, you bear up the bank into a short fenced path, beyond which you climb a stoney track to Laycock. Turn left along the road to Goose Eye; you can cut the corner by taking the first left, Roberts Street, where a stone-setted snicket down the back of the cottages runs down to rejoin the road.

Follow the road past The Turkey Inn in Goose Eye and, 100m up from the bridge, turn right on a signed path just past Rock Terrace. Cross the

wooden footbridge over the mill goit and continue past an old dam, on the obvious woodland path. Soon a paved section carries you out of the wood, rising above the stream past a long Pennine farmhouse, to turn left down a track, signed for Newsholme, to two old bridges – one a stone arch, the other an ancient clapper bridge, built from delicately balanced huge stone slabs.

Across the beck, head up the fence side to a gate, and up the hillside on the obvious path up Cat Clough. Along the path beyond the horse gate and stile at the top you soon reach a walled lane, into which you turn left down to Newsholme, bearing right on to a surfaced lane through the hamlet and past St John's Chapel. Don't miss Church Farm, with its old wind turbine. Part of the ornate building still functions as a church.

Cascading weirs along Dean Beck, near Goose Eye.

The lane crosses the valley to a T-junction. Bear right, then left up White Lane. As you crest the hill the view ahead is dominated by Ovenden Moor wind power station and Cock Hill, above Hebden Bridge, with Penistone Hill in the foreground. Haworth's church can just be seen, to the right of the solitary turbine at Haworth Brow.

The lane ends at a T-junction but your way lies ahead, down a grassy path which leads into a wide grassy lane, putting you on a track down to Pickles Hill.

Turn right along the road, then left through a white farm gate opposite a Variety Club of Great Britain cottage. Through the farmyard and the field gate beyond, you drop through meadows by a delightful stream. At a wooden stile turn left, along Hey Lane to a wooden ladder stile. Cross the rough track ahead, and follow the hedgeline down the field opposite to the the valley bottom where Long Bridge straddles the infant River Worth. This old packhorse bridge, which probably had earth ramps at either side to enable ponies to cross, served a route between Goose Eye and Haworth, following much the same line as you have just taken from Newsholme.

Take the lane on the opposite bank, over a stile, and continue uphill, right of an old sunken track, to a ladder stile and up the lane beyond to the Stanbury Road.

Turn left for 200m, then cross and take the flagged field path by the Brontë Parsonage sign, to pass (or visit if you wish) the museum and the church, then turning right down tourist-packed Main Street. At the bottom, walk down Bridgehouse Lane, across the railway bridge to turn right again. Past Bridgehouse Mills you'll find a snicket signed 'Uppergate, Oxenhope'; the obvious path follows a mill goit though fields, parallel to the railway.

Ignore the footbridge on the right and, past a derelict cottage, the path takes you, up a few steps, along a field edge to a gate. Pass Ives Bottom house and go through the gate beyond to bear immediately right, back to the stream. Past the old packhorse bridge, known as the Donkey Bridge, cross a metal footbridge and continue upstream.

Beyond a small water treatment works, go through a kissing gate on the right to cross another footbridge. Continuing upstream, the house above the fields on your right, Bents House, is better known as The Three Chimneys, home to the Railway Children in the classic film, much of which was shot in the area.

Eventually the path reaches a hard track. Turn right at The Barn into Mill Lane, over the beck then right, into Oxenhope Station for the train back to Keighley.

Steam train between Haworth and Oxenhope.

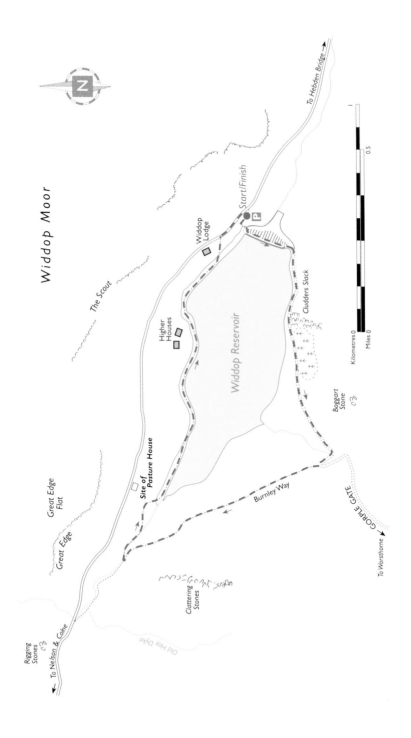

Widdop Moor

To Hebden Bridge

Start/Finish

Widdop Lodge

The Scout

Cludders Slack

Higher Houses

Widdop Reservoir

Boggart Stone

GORPLE GATE

To Worsthorne

Site of Pasture House

Great Edge Flat

Great Edge

Great Edge

Burnley Way

Clattering Stones

Old Hey Dyke

Rigging Stones

To Nelson & Colne

Kilometres 0

Miles 0

0.5

1

WIDDOP RESERVOIR

Of all the reservoirs in the South Pennines, be they for drinking water, powering mills or topping-up canals, Widdop is the most beautiful, set in a wide, crag-hemmed hollow and surrounded by mile after mile of rolling moorland. Poet Laureate Ted Hughes, who was born just a few miles away in Mytholmroyd in 1930, described it as a "frightened lake" in *Remains of Elmet*, his famous volume of poems about his vanishing South Pennine boyhood.

Widdop was, between 1871 and 1878, the first of the reservoirs to be built on the moors above Heptonstall, to supply drinking water for the people of Halifax. With a capacity of nearly 3000 million litres it's also the largest.

Materials for the dam that couldn't be found on site were brought along a horse-drawn tramway which ran from Shackleton, above the National Trust's main car park at Hardcastle Crags, along the edge of the Hebden valley to Holme End, Clough Foot and then Widdop. The materials were pulled up the hillside to Shackleton by a stationary engine on an inclined tramway, the huge ramp for which can be seen in the lower reaches of Crimsworth Dean. The tramline can still be traced on foot from Shackleton.

A gap in the car park wall, next to the information boards, puts you on the short, grassy path towards the reservoir wall, crossing a metal footbridge over the dam's spill channel. Turning left across the top of the embankment, you're confronted by the impressive gritstone outcrops of The Cludders, also known as Widdop Rocks, which are extremely popular with climbers of all ages and abilities. Other rock edges which form part of the hollow containing the reservoir have equally evocative names – Clattering Stones, Boggart Stones, Slack Stones and Frock Holes.

INFORMATION

Distance: 4.5 km (3 miles).

Start and finish: Car park, Widdop Reservoir, 8 km from Hebden Bridge on the Hebden Bridge to Colne road.

Terrain: Though a short, scenic walk, sections are on rough moorland and mud is unavoidable. Boots recommended.

Public transport: Nearest is the summer Sunday mini-bus service to Widdop Gate; there is a Mon-Sat service to Slack, 6km away, throughout the year

Refreshments: The Pack Horse pub is 1.5km south along the road, towards Hebden Bridge.

Note: The path along the north side of the dam is a permissive route provided by Yorkshire Water.

The view across the dam, from Cludders.

At the end of the dam wall take the track that bears right, past a small valve house. This is Gorple Gate, the old packhorse route which climbs out of Worsthorne towards Heptonstall, and is also encountered on Walk 14. The valve house looks slightly incongruous – an Egyptian building made from Pennine gritstone? Edward La Trobe Bateman, the engineer employed by Halifax Corporation to oversee the reservoir's construction, had attended the opening of the Suez Canal a year earlier and was impressed by the Egyptian architecture he saw there. The design of the valve house reflects the influence it had on him.

The waters edge on the south bank of Widdop Reservoir.

Walking along the track, you can't fail to notice the huge boulders scattered on the rough ground on your left, beneath Cludders. John Wesley, the Methodist preacher, is said to have delivered a sermon to Widdop's isolated population near here in 1766 – one of the stones is inscribed with his initials and the date.

After passing a small plantation, begin to climb gently away from the reservoir up a small clough, bearing right, across the small stream near the top. At a junction just above you'll find a Burnley Way marker post; turn right down the rough path which can be very muddy, though by way of compensation the view across the reservoir, of Great Edge below Widdop Moor, and of Wadsworth Moor, is quite exhilarating. On bright days in late summer/early autumn, when the bell heather and ling are in flower, the golden moor grasses are bathed in sunshine and the still waters of the dam reflect the clear blue sky, the scene is one of intense colour. Wildlife enthusiasts might be lucky enough to finds toads among the stones of the fallen wall at the pathside.

Walking the north bank of Widdop Reservoir.

At the foot of the path a wooden fingerpost directs you back towards the dam, over a wooden footbridge to a second finger-post at which you bear right. By a silt trap pond, where Old Hay Dyke's water flows into the dam, the path runs to the right of a wall for a few metres, then carries you over another footbridge and turns left, between the stone-lined water course and the reservoir.

Above you is yet another old packhorse route, between Heptonstall and Colne, now a surfaced road. Pasture House, on the roadside, was for many years known as the Traveller's Rest, moorland base for a gang of robbers who raided homes over the Lancashire border. The inn was itself raided and closed in 1891 for hosting an illegal gambling school.

Continuing along the path you pass the former reservoir keeper's house on your left; cross the water course on a short vehicle track which leads, through a metal gate, on to the road. Turn right down the tarmac for a short distance to return to the car park.

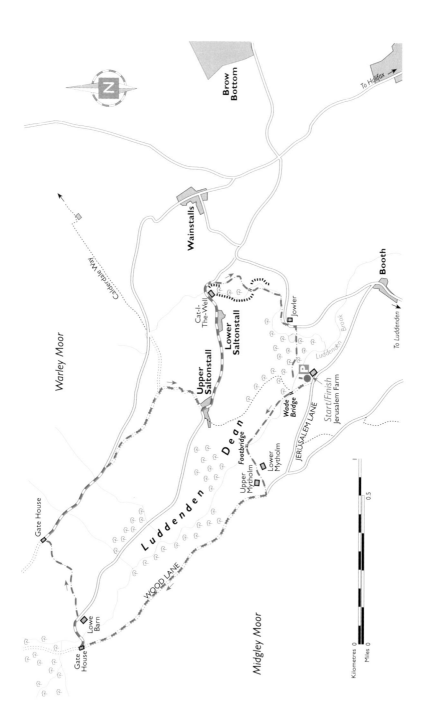

LUDDENDEN DEAN

Luddenden Dean is a tranquil gem, tucked away in a corner of Calderdale with only limited access by road. There is a small population – a few scattered farms and cottages, and the picturesque hamlet of Saltonstall – together with a country pub, the Cat'I'The'Well Inn which, despite its remote location, is rarely quiet.

Through a gate at the foot of the car park, a track leads down to Wade Bridge which spans Luddenden Brook. Wade Wood, in which you now stand, is a Site of Special Scientific Interest; among the oak, birch, beech and rowan, holly, hazel, bilberry and numerous wild flowers and grasses are indicators that this could be ancient woodland, looking much as it would have in the wake of the last Ice Age.

Across the stone-arched bridge head upstream on the right bank, over a stile, and take the path ahead to the left, down the bank. This path follows the streamside, at one point using the bedrock as a path; when the stream is swollen this could be impassable but it is easily avoided by taking a path to your right up the bank, then dropping back almost immediately. Kingfishers and herons are frequently seen along the stream.

Mullioned windows and the picturesque terraced gardens at Upper Mytholm.

INFORMATION

Distance: 7.5 km (4.5 miles).

Start and finish: Jerusalem Farm, near Booth, best reached by leaving the A646 at Luddenden Foot, following the sign to Booth. Drive through Booth and take the first left, Jerusalem Lane, immediately after a sharp, steep bend in the road – don't miss the turning as manoeuvring your car round to return and take the bend will prove difficult. Jerusalem Farm is 800m further on the right. This is the only car park in the valley.

Terrain: Delightful, undemanding stream-side paths and quiet country lanes.

Public transport: Buses from Halifax and Sowerby Bridge stop at Booth, 800m from Jerusalem Farm.

Refreshments: The Cat-I-The-Well Inn.

Opening hours: Jerusalem Farm car park is open 0800-2200. Calderdale Countryside Service run a series of activities and courses here; details from 01422 359454.

Continued on next page.

Note: While there are no rights of way through Castle Carr Estate, Calderdale Countryside Service leads an annual guide walk through the area, by permission of the landowner, during which the magnificent fountains are usually given their once-yearly blow-through.

Over a wooden footbridge head uphill, towards the small clough between Lower and Upper Mytholm Farms. The magnificent terraced garden of the latter is best viewed from this side of the clough. Upper Mytholm, originally a farm, has retained its distinctive mullioned windows which let light into the weavers' rooms on the upper floor. Stay on the left bank of the clough, over a stile and through a gate, up to Wood Lane, along which you turn right for 1.5km, to pass through the impressive gatehouse for the Castle Carr Estate.

The estate, through which there are no public paths, was established by Captain Joseph Priestley Edwards in the mid-1800s. After buying up large areas he set about building a mansion of breathtaking opulence. Long driveways led to a courtyard with a coach house for half a dozen carriages. The entrance was a Norman archway, with portcullis, and inside was a huge banqueting hall with an oak-framed ceiling. The grounds were laid out around a series of reservoirs with five fountains, the highest of which flung water 40m into the air – said at the time to be the highest in Europe. Edwards died in a railway disaster before the house was finished, and successive owners found the estate too expensive to maintain. The house was demolished in the 1960s.

Following the lane over the bridge you reach, opposite Lowe Barn, stone steps in the wall on your left. The path beyond zigzags uphill, following wooden markers through rough pasture and across a field to a stile. Heading across the next field towards the right-hand corner of the farm building ahead,

Waterfalls beneath Caty Well Bridge.

you emerge in Castle Carr Road by a second, equally impressive gatehouse.

Turn right here, and right again at the junction 500m further on, beyond two old railway trucks, down a rough lane. Turn right at the second fork, down the Calderdale Way through Upper Saltonstall. Saltonstall was a Norman vaccary, or cattle ranch, until the early 14th century when it was split up and let to local farmers who ploughed the pastures to grow oats. At the foot of the lane turn left, past Great House along the surfaced lane to Lower Saltonstall and, just beyond, the Cat-I-The-Well inn.

Past the pub, cross Caty Well Bridge and take the next track off to the right, down to a wicket gate, to follow a concrete path in front of a row of terraced cottages. Go left at the bottom, in front of Grotto

Mill pond at Jowler.

Terrace, where the path follows concrete flags into a small wooded clough. Ford the stream here carefully – the bedrock is smooth and slippery, and the opposite bank is muddy. Climb the opposite bank but not the wire fence at the top; the path runs left, between the stream and the fence, to a small stone bridge by a cottage. Cross this and follow the track uphill, past the mill pond, forking left near the top, on to the stone-surfaced road at Jowler.

Just down the road you'll find a path on the right, signed for Jerusalem Farm, which drops down wooden steps into Wade Wood and crosses another mill pond. The surfaced path will lead you to a row of stepping stones over Luddenden Brook and the meadows below Jerusalem Farm; the car park is a short, steep climb up the grassy bank.

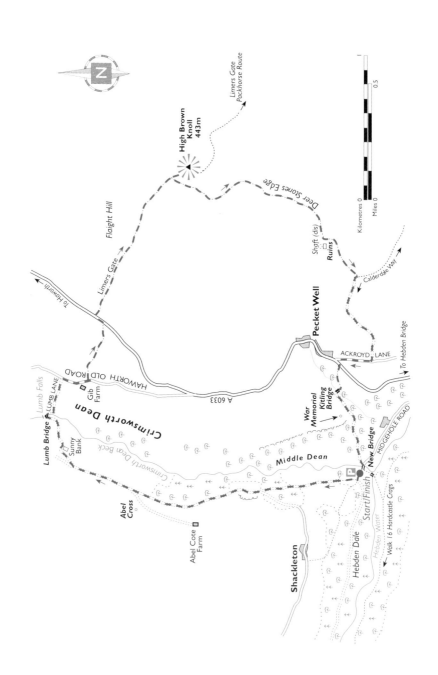

High Brown Knoll 443m

Limers Gate Packhorse Route

Flaight Hill

Limers Gate

To Haworth

Deer Stones Edge

Shaft (dis)

Ruins

Calderdale Way

Pecket Well

ACKROYD LANE

To Hebden Bridge

HAWORTH OLD ROAD

Gib Farm

A 6033

Lumb Falls

LUMB LANE

Crimsworth Dean

Lumb Bridge

Sunny Bank

Crimsworth Dean Beck

War Memorial

Kitling Bridge

MIDGEHOLE ROAD

Middle Dean

Abel Cross

Abel Cote Farm

New Bridge

Start/Finish

P

Hebden Dale

Hebden Water

Walk 16 Hardcastle Crags

Shackleton

Kilometres 0

Miles 0

0.5

LUMB FALLS AND HIGH BROWN KNOLL

rimsworth Dean is every bit as beautiful as its adjacent sister, the Hebden Valley. Its beauty, however, comes not from semi-planted woodlands like those up the Hebden, but from a wilder, moorland aspect. Its rough, grazed slopes are home to hares, pheasant and occasionally partridge, while sparrowhawks can be seen flitting among the trees in the bottom. Scattered stone farmsteads, many in ruins, dot the springlines on the valley sides like jet beads on a necklace and the ancient Limers Gate packhorse route climbs, from a beautiful waterfall, high on to the moors above.

As you climb the steps, right of the National Trust information caravan at New Bridge, keep your eyes open. Woodpeckers can often be seen here, along with bullfinch, robins and wrens, and herons, flying up the valley to quieter fishing grounds.

As you climb the surfaced track up the valley, past Hollin Hall, the Trust's estate base, and through a stand of tall pines, look out for long-tailed tit and red squirrels. Though the latter are close to extinction, there are still occasional sightings.

Leaving Trust-owned land just after a cattle grid, you reach the driveway for Abel Cote Farm. A

INFORMATION

Distance: 12 km (7.5 miles).

Start and finish: Hardcastle Crags car park, Midgehole, Hebden Bridge.

Terrain: This is a very varied route, through woodland, along ancient packhorse trails and open moorland. High Brown Knoll can be a wild spot in poor weather. Boots and waterproofs strongly recommended.

Public transport: Mini-buses from Hebden Bridge serve Hardcastle Crags every day except Sunday.

Refreshments: The Robin Hood at Pecket Well. As this comes towards the end of the walk, you should carry a drink and snacks.

Note: The National Trust charges for parking. An honesty system operates when the car park is unattended. In poor weather route finding on High Brown Knoll can be difficult; OS map and compass are essential.

The unusual twin-headed Abel Cross, Crimsworth Dean.

short detour along this track, no more than 200m, brings you to Abel Cross, an unusual twin-headed monument which, according to legend, marks the spot where two would-be suitors were buried after killing each other during a duel over a local farm girl. It's more likely that the cross was in fact a monastic boundary marker.

Return to the main track and continue up the valley. About 800m past the next farm turn right, down a waymarked bridleway, past ruined Sunnybank Farm to Lumb Hole.

Here Crimsworth Dean Beck tumbles over Lumb Falls into an idyllic, tree-shaded shallow pool above which Lumb Bridge carries the ancient Limers Gate packhorse route. Centuries ago hardy Galloway ponies would have crossed the bridge bearing cargoes of lime between Lancashire and Yorkshire, to be used to sweeten agricultural pastures.

Cross the bridge and turn right, up Lumb Lane, which climbs to the Haworth Old Road. Turn right on the tarmac, then left after Gib Farm. The waymarked bridleway passes through two gates then bears right to climb a rough field to the A6033 Haworth to Hebden Bridge road. Limers Gate continues through a wooden gate, 70m up the road on the opposite side.

After a kilometre the narrow moorland path leads you to the trig pillar on High Brown Knoll, an excellent place to admire the view across the Brontë moors to Boulsworth, Pendle, Black Hameldon and Stoodley Pike. Sweeping round from the TV mast on Windy Hill you can see Emley Moor transmitter and the chimneys at Queensbury, home of the famous Black Dyke Mills brass band.

From the trig pillar, head south to Deer Stones Edge, following a series of marker posts across the moor which eventually follow a ditch leading to a more obvious path along the moor edge. At a crossroads of paths, past a small quarry, angle steeply right, diagonally downhill almost parallel to the descending ditch on your right, to the ruins of Weather House and an airshaft. Keep left of the enclosed field by the ruins and beyond stick to the obvious track to another disused quarry, after which it switchbacks sharp right, along the moor edge wall, to a walled lane which carries the Calderdale Way downhill. At the bottom head straight across, bearing slightly left down a path which can be somewhat overgrown and damp at its lower end.

The lane carries you down to a small collection of cottages. Turn right, down the lane in front of them, to Ackroyd Lane. Turn right again here, following the Calderdale Way signs – the small village ahead is Pecket Well, home to Britain's only surviving mill producing fustian (a coarse cotton fabric used in corduroy) and, more usefully, the Robin Hood Inn. After 300 m, if you are not going into Pecket Well, turn left down a step through the wall. This short path brings you down to cross the A6033 and opposite, the dusty Calderdale Way carries you into Pecket Well Clough.

Lunb Falls, beneath the Limers Gate packhorse track.

A short distance down the path a wider, paved track on the right crosses Kitling packhorse bridge into National Trust-managed beech woods. This leafy lane drops through the woods to emerge conveniently into Midgehole Road behind the public toilets, near the car park entrance.

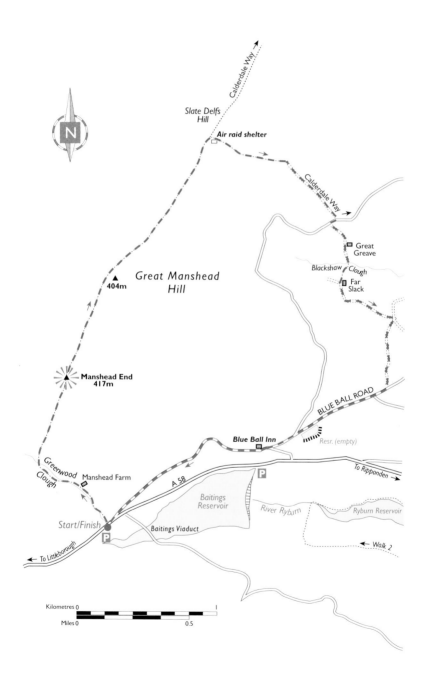

N

Calderdale Way

Slate Delfs
Hill

Air raid shelter

Calderdale Way

Great
Greave

Blackshaw Clough

Far
Slack

Great Manshead
Hill

▲
404m

✷ Manshead End
417m

BLUE BALL ROAD

Resr. (empty)

Blue Ball Inn

Greenwood
Clough

Manshead Farm

To Ripponden

A 58

P

Baitings
Reservoir

River Ryburn

Ryburn Reservoir

Start/Finish

P

Baitings Viaduct

Walk 2

To Littleborough

Kilometres 0   1

Miles 0   0.5

GREAT MANSHEAD

Great Manshead is a hillwalker's hill. From the airy summit cairn at Manshead End a gentle, descending path follows the broad grassy ridge giving extensive views across Turley Holes and Higher Head Moor and the Calder Valley.

Until 1993 walkers could only dream about the route's quality. There had been no paths on the hill, used for sheep grazing and some shooting. Then, following extensive consultations Calderdale Council's Countryside Service, with funding from Yorkshire Water, created the new 3.5km path along the ridge, linking into the Calderdale Way and the footpath network in the Cragg Vale area.

Your starting point lies practically at the foot of Manshead. Cross the road to climb the ladder stile opposite, signed for Manshead Hill and Waterstalls Road. Crossing a footbridge beyond puts you up a banking to a marker board, pointing left.

The volunteers and full-time countryside staff who created the path have done a thorough job and a detailed description is unnecessary. The path, always evident on the ground, heads up Greenhead Clough past Manshead Farm on your right – strategic marker posts guide your way and new footbridges have been placed where needed.

INFORMATION

Distance: 9 km (5.5 miles).

Start and finish: Layby on the A58 Rochdale Road, 4km west of Ripponden at the western end of Baitings Reservoir.

Terrain: From rough pasture to high moor, plus quiet farm tracks and country lanes. In poor weather this walk should only be attempted by properly equipped, experienced walkers. Boots and waterproofs essential.

Public transport: Buses from Halifax, Littleborough and Rochdale should stop at the start point if requested.

Refreshments: The Blue Ball Inn is near the end of the walk. A snack van can occasionally be found in the layby at the start.

Note: There is an information board in the layby. Dogs are not permitted on Manshead, nor are organised walking and running events.

The summit of Manshead End.

Beyond Manshead Farm the path leaves the walled intake fields and an easy step over a new fence delivers you on to the open moor. The yellow-topped marker posts which guide you uphill seem hardly necessary – just keep going until you can't climb any further! This is the steepest part of the walk, particularly tough if you're ascending against a north wind.

Looking east towards the Ryburn Valley.

The view from the summit (417m/1,368ft) is one of the best in the South Pennines, and in a land of fine viewpoints that's saying something; to the south, beyond Rishworth Moor, the dark, featureless plateaux of the Peak National Park blacken the horizon. South-west, rugged Blackstone Edge carries the Pennine Way along the watershed at its narrowest point, and to the west the moors around Rawtenstall and Todmorden seem to go on for ever. To the north are Midgeley, Widdop and Heptonstall Moors.

Follow the marker posts from the summit cairn, along Great Manshead Hill (404m), for 2km. Mesolithic hunter-gatherers probably used this route thousands of years ago to avoid the dangerous, swamp and beast-infested wooded valley floors. Flint implements have been found on the slopes of the hill, along with Bronze Age tools.

Bear right on meeting a wallside track, for 400m, to the brick air-raid shelter on Slate Delfs Hill. The building is a curious reminder of the last war. A handful of men stationed here lit up the hillside during German bombing raids, in the hope that the pilots would mistake the lights for nearby Halifax and drop their deadly cargoes harmlessly on to the moor; a nerve-racking posting.

Turn right, past the shelter, along the Calderdale Way for a brief flirtation east. Follow the rough track for 150m, then climb a step stile on your left, by a marker post, to head diagonally across a small patch of rough moor. The embankment of the Flints Dam beyond brings you to a wooden step stile and into a lane down to Greave Road. Here you leave the Calderdale Way, turning right for 50m, then left into the lane signed to Blackshaw Clough. Drop down the lane, to the very front of Great Greave Farm.

The right of way turns right, along the house front, then down the side, where a waymarker guides you into a muddy, overgrown lane, to cross the Blackshaw Clough brook and climb up to Far Slack Farm. There, go through the wooden gate on the left side of farm buildings, and straight across the farmyard, through a white steel gate ahead, into Slack Lane. Follow this for 500m to a junction, where you turn right, up a grassy walled bridleway to Blue Ball Road.

Turn right along the tarmac – the lane, which might once have been part of the Roman Road over Blackstone Edge, is usually quiet and the views ahead, of Baitings dam, Rishworth Moor and initially Manshead End, are enough to take your mind off the hard surface. You soon reach the Blue Ball Inn, an old packhorse inn pre-dating the A58 turnpike road to which the lane eventually returns you – the layby is just across the road.

The old packhorse inn near journey's end.

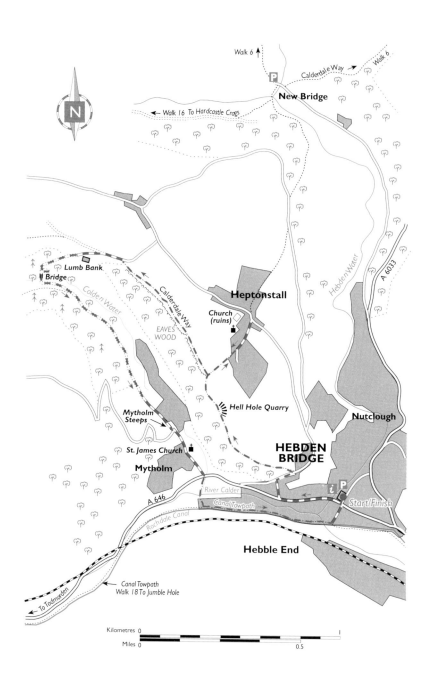

Walk 6

Calderdale Way

Walk 6

New Bridge

← Walk 16 To Hardcastle Crags

N

Lumb Bank
Bridge

Colden Water

Calderdale Way

Heptonstall

Church
(ruins)

Hebden Water

A 6033

EAVES
WOOD

Hell Hole Quarry

Nutclough

Mytholm
Steeps

St. James Church

**HEBDEN
BRIDGE**

Mytholm

A 646

River Calder

Canal Towpath

i P

Start/Finish

Rochdale Canal

Hebble End

To Todmorden

Canal Towpath
Walk 18 To Jumble Hole

Kilometres 0 _____ 1
Miles 0 _____ 0.5

HEPTONSTALL AND THE LOWER COLDEN VALLEY

eptonstall, perched on the hillside above Hebden Bridge, is one of the oldest settlements in the South Pennines. This was a thriving handloom weavers' village before the textile industry migrated to the valley floor, and among the ancient buildings to be found in the village is the Cloth Hall, built in the mid-16th century, to which 'pieces' of cloth (a 'piece' was 30 yards long) were brought by packhorse from across the South Pennines to be sold. For a hundred years or more this was the only such hall in the South Pennines, pre-dating Halifax's grandiose Piece Hall by more than 200 years.

There are many fascinating buildings in the village. The octagonal Methodist chapel, reached off Northgate, was built in 1764, the foundation stone being laid by the non-conformist preacher John Wesley; the ruined church of St Thomas à Becket was first recorded around 1260 and closed after storm damage in 1847 – the grave of Cragg Vale coiner David Hartley is just 10 m from its porch.

With so much to explore, it's worth picking up a copy of the village trail booklet before leaving the information centre in Hebden Bridge, and allowing extra time to take in the village sights.

INFORMATION

Distance: 8 km (5 miles).

Start and finish: Tourist Information Centre, Hebden Bridge.

Terrain: Woodland paths, old stone setts and easy bridleways.

Public transport: Hebden Bridge is well served by trains on the York-Blackpool coast-to-coast service, as well as local services from Leeds, Bradford, Littleborough and Manchester Piccadilly. Buses to Hebden Bridge from Keighley, Halifax, Rochdale and Burnley.

Refreshments: Hebden Bridge has everything from restaurants and teashops to an excellent curry house and several pubs.

Opening hours: Heptonstall Grammar School Museum has displays relating to local history, including a small collection of tools used by David Hartley's Cragg Vale Coiners (Walk 12). Opening hours are limited: contact 01484 719222 for details.

The old packhorse bridge over Hebden Water, Hebden Bridge.

To start the walk, go along Market Street and after crossing Hangingroyd Road turn right into Stoney Lane, up a flight of stone steps to Heptonstall Road. Turn right there and cross to take the track signed 'Hell Hole Rocks and Heptonstall 1'. Hell Hole quarry is reached after a few hundred metres. Today its sheer, overhanging walls are popular with climbers and it is said that an underground passage leads beneath the quarry wall under the hillside, to Tom Bell's Cave, mentioned in Walk 16. As with all such legends, his treasure is said to be sealed in the passage; it is also said that the robber could hear the church bells at Mytholm through the passage.

At the far end of the quarry, the path bears right, rounding a huge, leaning black boulder, up a flight of zig-zag steps to the top of Eaves Wood. There a walled path on the right leads, through a new housing estate, to Heptonstall.

Having explored the village and perhaps refreshed yourself in one of its two pubs, retrace your steps to Eaves Wood and turn right on the Calderdale Way, along the edge of the crags at the top of the wood; ignore the paths leading down into the wood. After 800 m you emerge into Green Lane, and turn left. You are still on the Calderdale Way but this soon branches off to the right, while you continue downhill on the tarmac. This ends at the entrance to Lumb Bank, home of the Arvon Foundation.

The 18th century mill owner's house was once home to the poet Ted Hughes. In 1975 he returned to Devon, where he became involved with the Foundation, established in 1972 to enable established and budding wordsmiths to practise their art under professional guidance. Hughes leased and later sold Mill Bank to the Foundation, which now has three such centres, the others being in Devon, and Scotland.

The small sheds in front of the house are writing cabins, in which writers can find solitude and hopefully, helped by the beautiful views of the Colden Valley, a little inspiration.

The old church of
St Thomas a Becket,
Heptonstall.

After 250 m the track sweeps round in front of
Lumb Cottages, to cross Colden Water on a stone
parapetted bridge. This is the site of Lower Lumb
Mill, its chimney built directly on to the rock in
the stream bed. Across the bridge follow the track
left, as it gently climbs to join the main Colden
Valley bridleway through oakwoods, where you
might hear or even catch a glimpse of brightly
coloured jays screeching among the foliage.

Looking up the Colden
Valley.

Follow the bridleway down the valley
for a kilometre; it ends on the steep,
winding tarmac road known locally as
Mytholm Steeps. Turn left here, past
St James' Church, down to the A646.
Cross the main road and pass through
a gap in the wall opposite, down steps
to a path which follows the last few
metres of Colden Water as it flows
into the River Calder. A metal
footbridge carries you over the river,
and heading up the side of Stubbing
Square you will find yourself on the
Rochdale Canal towpath. Turning
left, pass Stubbing Locks and walk
over the aqueduct, back into Hebden
Bridge; a stone head on the side of
the bridge, hard to spot unless you
lean well over, gazes up towards the
confluence of the Calder with
Hebden Water.

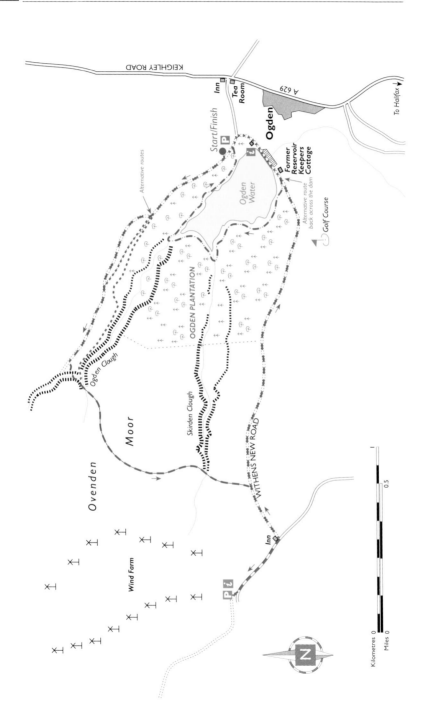

KEIGHLEY ROAD

Inn

Tea Room

A 629

Ogden

To Halifax

Start/Finish

Alternative routes

Ogden Water

Former Reservoir Keepers Cottage

Alternative route back across the dam

Golf Course

OGDEN PLANTATION

Ogden Clough

Skirden Clough

M o o r

O v e n d e n

WITHENS NEW ROAD

Inn

Wind Farm

N

Kilometres 0
Miles 0
0.5

OGDEN WATER

The woods and moorland around Ogden Water have provided the people of Halifax with a rural retreat for many years. The 1000 million litre dam was constructed across the confluence of Ogden and Skirden cloughs, source of the Hebble Brook which flows through Halifax, between 1854 and 1857 to supply the town with its daily needs of water.

Calderdale Council's Leisure Services Department entered into a management agreement for the area with Yorkshire Water in 1987. It has had a full-time countryside officer and a team of volunteer rangers on site since then. Paths suitable for the disabled have been constructed and an orienteering course has been developed.

Footbridge in the dry stone walling display area.

This short, usually undemanding walk is a weekend favourite and boasts surprising variety, from the wooded water's edge to the open moor. It has everything, including West Yorkshire's highest pub, conveniently positioned at the half-way stage, and a rich variety of birdlife.

Rock Hollow car park is a good place to begin the walk, especially when the rhododendron on the bank below is in flower. Start through the gate at the far end of the lower car park and follow the

INFORMATION

Distance: 7 km (4.5 miles).

Start and finish: Rock Hollow car park, Ogden Water, off the A629 Keighley Road from Halifax.

Terrain: Very varied. In poor weather the short moorland stretch can be a serious undertaking. Boots and waterproofs recommended.

Public transport: Buses from Halifax, Haworth, Bradford and Huddersfield stop at Causeway Foot.

Refreshments: There is a pub, called the Whole Hog at the time of writing, and the Rock Hollow Tea Rooms at the junction with Ogden Lane and Halifax Road, not far from the start. The Withens Pub, at the halfway stage, is the highest pub in West Yorkshire.

Opening hours: Rock Hollow car park: Jan-Feb, Nov-Dec 0800-1700; Mar-Apr, Sep-Oct 0800-1900; May and Aug 0800-2100; Jun-Jul 0800-2200 (in emergencies telephone 01422 365101). Ogden Visitor Centre: Sat-Sun 1000-1600.

Continued on next page.

Notes: The temptation to take a dip in the reservoir on warm summer days is great but should be resisted. The water is deep, still and even at the height of summer remains ice cold a short way out from the edge. Two teenagers drowned here in summer 1996. Dogs should be kept on leads around the reservoir; there is a dog toilet in the woods near the car park.

track beyond. On the right side of the track, after 200m, you'll find a dry stone walling display area, with examples of stiles and types of walling – there's even a shooting butt. Some 100m beyond, the track veers right. You have a choice here: follow the fence on your left, up the clough; continue along the track right, well above the clough; or keep straight ahead, along a faint rough grassland path which passes a wooden and a concrete post, then follows a collapsed wall, to a metal gate, where it rejoins the track.

Whichever option you choose, after just over a kilometre you'll find a flight of stone steps which descends into the clough (if you opted for the fence you should already be in the clough!). There you can cross the stream. Up another flight of steps on the opposite bank, and over a wooden stile, you reach the edge of Ovenden Moor.

The whirling blades of Ovenden Moor wind power station.

The obvious path, marked by posts and small cairns, heads across the moor below the 23 wind turbines of Ovenden Moor. The moor is home to several species of ground nesting birds including wheatear, red grouse, curlew and skylark.

Another silt trap carries you across Skirden Clough, one of Ogden's main feeders, beyond which you can stride out along a flagged track to a stile. Turn right here, up Withens New Road, for the Withens pub and then right, along the road beyond for 400m to the small car park and information boards at Ovenden Moor wind power station, whose 32 metre-high turbine towers are said by Yorkshire Windpower to produce enough energy for 7,500 homes.

The Top Withens Hotel, the highest pub in West Yorkshire.

Wind 'farms' have in recent years stirred up fierce environmental debates in the South Pennines. When Ovenden Moor was proposed there was little resistance. But a rash of applications for larger developments since has raised fears that the area's upland beauty could be lost to a sea of spinning blades. Well-organised campaigns have, so far, seen off plans for further moorland power stations.

Return to the pub – in which wind power is doubtless a topic hotly debated over many a pint – and go back through the kissing gate at the side of the building to head down Withens New Road alongside an element-battered golf course, across which you have a good view of Halifax. The track leads back to the reservoir, a distance of about 1.5km.

Here you can either cross the dam to the car park or, opposite the former reservoir keeper's cottage, go through a kissing gate and follow the obvious path to complete a delightful circuit of the reservoir. The path, which keeps close to the water's edge at times and at others meanders along the woodland floor, eventually brings you back to the car park. The variety of waterfowl on the dam is gradually increasing – you might see goosanders, sandpipers and dippers on and around the water, as well as great spotted and green woodpeckers among the trees. Flocks of crossbills have been known to feed among the larch and conifers, and short-eared owls roost in the trees near the moor.

Kilometres 0
Miles 0
0.5

To Glusburn

Holme Beck

A 6068 COLNE ROAD

Lund's Tower

Earl Crag

Wainman's Pinnacle

Hitching Stone

Lane Ends Farm

Wainman's Bottoms

Footbridge

Lane Ends

Carr Head Hall

Footbridge

Baywood House Farm

Fold Barn

Ickornshaw Beck

Sykeside

Cowling

OLD LANE

Gill Beck

CINDER HILL LANE

GILL LANE

Cowling Hill

Start/Finish

Ickornshaw

A 6068

To Colne

EARL CRAG AND THE HITCHING STONE

During the 18th century, South Pennine Man seems to have had a curious habit of building hill-top monuments, the most famous being Stoodley Pike above Todmorden. Earl Crag, a ridge of outcropping gritstone west of the Aire Valley, boasts not one but two such monuments, their inspiration as confusing as their names. But on the moor behind the crag there's a natural monument which might itself serve to remind us that nature will never be dominated.

You'll find Cinder Hill Lane next to Holy Trinity Church in Cowling, signed for Wainman's Bottoms. It leads you, past a TV mast, through a wicket gate by an old field gate and along the top of the small wood above Ickornshaw Beck. It drops in front of Wood Farm, through a field gate to the beck side. Within 150m, near the confluence of the beck with Gill Beck, you cross a long footbridge and turn right, through a kissing gate by a field gate, along Ickornshaw Beck. In the second field you pass a small kiln, below the splendid Carr Head Hall.

INFORMATION

Distance: 11km (7 miles).

Start and finish: Holy Trinity Church, Gill Lane, Cowling.

Terrain: Varied; the optional diversion to the Hitching Stone can be muddy. Boots recommended.

Public transport: Buses from Keighley, Nelson and Colne.

Refreshments: None on route but Cowling has several inns and a chip shop.

The Lime Kiln by Ickornshaw Beck, below Carr Head Hall.

Cross the next footbridge, at Wainman's Bottoms, and walk 100 m up the lane on the other side into Lane Ends Farm. You don't need to enter the farmyard – go through the field gate on your right, up the side of the barn and directly up the field to the gate ahead. This is not a right of way but the farmer has no objection to the route being taken as long as sensible behaviour is observed.

Through the gate turn left for 10 m, then cross the A6068 to climb stone steps over the wall. Head up the field, as though towards castellated Lund's Tower on the crag ahead, until you see another step stile in the wall ahead. Cross this and walk straight up the fields ahead, with the wall on your right. You soon go through a kissing gate to enter a muddy walled lane, which is crossed further up by a farm track. Beyond, the lane is impassable but you can easily avoid it by walking up the scrub moorland on its right, to a metalled lane.

Wainman's Pinnacle, known locally as Cowling Pinnacle.

The lane offers the gentlest way up to Earl Crag. After 800 m of calf-building ascent a rough track, just below Lund's Tower, switches back on the right up to the tower.

Lund's Tower – also called Jubilee Tower or Ethel's Tower – is known locally as Sutton Pinnacle. No-one is quite sure whether James Lund built it to mark Queen Victoria's Golden Jubilee in 1887 or the birth of his daughter Ethel. A flight of 39 steps leads up the interior to a small platform, which offers fine views of the Yorkshire Dales, Rombald's Moor, and Pendle to the west.

Follow the crag edge over three stiles to Wainman's Pinnacle, known locally as Cowling Pinnacle. Most believe it marked the Battle of Waterloo in 1815, but it's also said that it was built by Richard Wainman of Carr Head, whose wife was afflicted with the 'evil eye'; whatever she saw first from her window each morning would be dogged by bad luck all day. Wainman built the tower so that it would be the first thing she saw – the 'eye' having no effect on stone.

A worthwhile detour can be made from here to the Hitching Stone. Simply follow the wall-side track from the tower to cross the lane beyond. Through the stile opposite follow the wall south for a kilometre; when the path is muddy the stones on the ground by the wall will help keep your boots clean.

The Hitching Stone is thought to be Yorkshire's largest detached boulder and weighs an estimated 1,000 tons. Legend says it once stood on Rombald's Moor, in front of a witch's house. One day, in a fit, she took her broomstick and flipped – or hitched – it across the valley to where it stands today.

Retrace your steps to Wainman's Pinnacle and turn left along Earl Crag for 100 m, to a path which drops down the heather slopes to the lane below. The area is

The Hitching Stone with its cell-like Priest's Chair.

crossed by dozens of sheep tracks, but all serve your purpose. Wherever you emerge on the lane, turn left to Baywood House Farm (marked Baildon on the OS map), go up the drive and turn right into a field. Follow the right side of the field, through a step stile and across the next field into a walled lane which brings you to Barley Croft.

Turn left, between Fold Barn and Sykeside, then right, along the fence behind Sykeside, down a slippery bank and over a small stream. Cross the next field to a gate and follow the left hand side of the next two fields to Farling Ing Top, leaving the final field by a gate. Follow the track ahead to turn right, down the lane, back to Cowling. At the bottom cross the A6068 and head down Gill Lane, opposite, to return to the church.

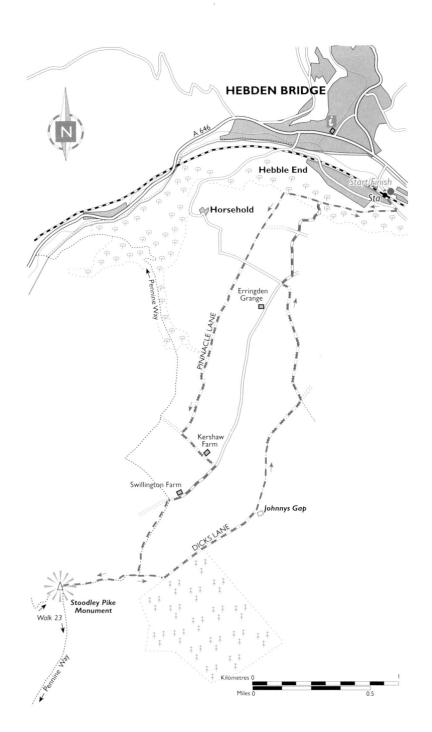

STOODLEY PIKE FROM HEBDEN BRIDGE

If a graphic designer was asked to design a corporate logo for the South Pennines then Stoodley Pike's pointed black monument would undoubtedly feature. The first Stoodley Pike monument was a chimney-shaped obelisk, built in 1815 to commemorate the Peace of Ghent and the abdication of Napoleon a year earlier. So in reality it's a peace memorial, rather than a war memorial as many suppose. It collapsed in 1854 when the Crimean War broke out, to be rebuilt two years later when peace was declared, and then suffered a partial collapse the day before the end of World War I in November 1918.

From the booking office at picturesque Hebden Bridge Railway Station, a short path to your right leads down to Station Road, to turn right under the railway bridge. Past the end of Palace House Road, 10m up the lane opposite, a sharp turn right puts you on a concrete track which soon becomes a grassy lane, climbing into Crow Nest Wood from where there are good views across Hebden Bridge of the 'top and bottom' houses which cling to the hillside.

A good 600m up the path a wicket gate leads you into the top corner of the wood, bluebell-carpeted

INFORMATION

Distance: 11 km (7 miles).

Start and finish: Hebden Bridge Railway Station.

Terrain: Woodland, field and moorland paths, easy going underfoot with only a small amount of mud. Boots and waterproofs recommended.

Public transport: Hebden Bridge is well served by trains on the York-Blackpool coast to coast service, and local services from Leeds, Bradford, Littleborough and Manchester Piccadilly. It can be reached by bus from Keighley, Haworth, Halifax, Todmorden, Rochdale and Burnley.

Refreshments: Cafes, pubs, shops and restaurants in Hebden Bridge.

Note: This walk can be combined with Walk 23, Stoodley Pike from Todmorden, to make a lengthy figure of eight.

Hebden Bridge's 'top and bottom' houses.

in spring, through which an obvious path takes you past a TV mast and over a stone step stile to cross New Road. The wicket gate opposite puts you on a field edge path at the top of which you enter Pinnacle Lane, through a steel gate. The lane, which passes through the neatly laid-out walls and fields of Erringden Grange model farm, seems to head directly for Stoodley Pike. It leads straight on for a kilometre, its line evident even where parts of the walls are missing.

The line is broken when, through a wicket gate by a steel field gate, you turn left, up a dusty lane past Kershaw Farm. At the end, turn right on Kilnshaw Lane, then through the gate by Swillington Farm. Just beyond, a fingerpost directs you left, up the moor along the Pennine Way.

The Public Slake Trough on the Pennine Way near Stoodley Pike.

The well-trodden route climbs to a ladder stile and goes right, through a gap stile, to head directly for Stoodley Pike. On the way keep an eye out for the 'Public Slaketrough', a stone trough at the side of the path into which flows clear spring water – its name, carved on the trough, is now indiscernible.

Stoodley Pike monument stands a short distance beyond the trough. A major landmark for Pennine Wayfarers, for whom it never seems to get any closer as they approach from the south, it overlooks Todmorden and the Lancashire hills beyond and on a clear day the view from the stone balcony halfway up extends a long way in every direction. There might have been an ancient burial mound on the site; it is said that when workmen began to lay the foundations in 1815, lightning erupted from the ground and human bones were found.

To reach the balcony you'll have to climb the 40 steps inside the monument, feeling your way in the dark (it's worth carrying a torch) – beware of sheep sheltering from the elements on the staircase.

Having climbed the pike to admire the view, retrace your steps past the Slaketrough and through the gap stile. Ignore the step stile, heading instead for a broad walled lane by a plantation. This is Dick's Lane and it takes you to the ruined farm known as Johnny's Gap. In the mid 19th century an annual fair was held here by tenant farmers – it's hard to believe today, given the wonderfully exposed nature of the site and the fact that the ruin is little more than a pile of stones.

Following the sign for Rake Head, turn left out of the lane, along the wallside, ignoring a junction on the left. Nearly a kilometre from Johnny's Gap, after the bumpy lane has become an unexpected green swathe, turn left over a stile by a five-bar gate, into the lane past Rake Head, the old Erringden Township workhouse.

The dusty track drops to a crossroads. Your way is right, bearing left after 100 m, down the walled lane which goes straight through the next crossroads to pass under a small bridge carrying another path over your head – note the absence of mortar in the construction – back into Crow Nest Wood. Follow the path left, down to the wicket gate encountered on the outward journey. Turn right there and retrace your steps to the station.

The Rochdale Canal,
Hebden Bridge.

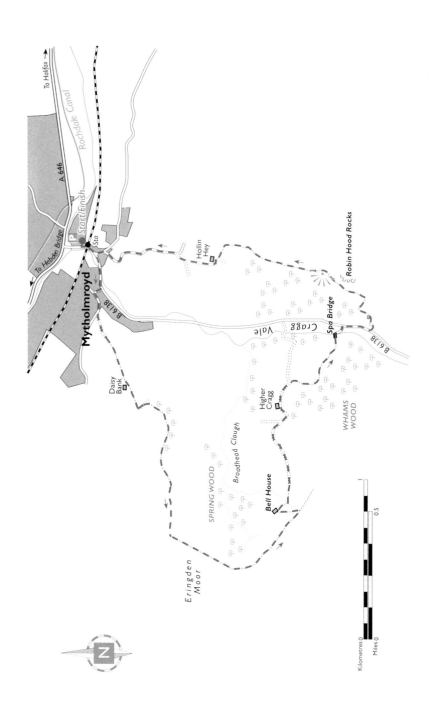

THE CRAGG VALE COINERS

I n the 18th century many Cragg Vale farms were home to a notorious gang of counterfeiters led by David Hartley, whose activities won him the nickname 'King David'. Mytholmroyd innkeepers, sometimes coerced, provided the gang with their raw materials – coins, from which they clipped the edges to melt down and stamp into fake currency. Those same landlords then put them into circulation, passing them as change in the dimly-lit taverns.

In 1769 Government excise man William Deighton was sent to investigate and had several coiners, including Hartley, arrested. Deighton paid for this interference with his life but many more coiners were soon caught. Deighton's murderers and Hartley were hanged in York and their corpses hung on Beacon Hill above Halifax, as a warning to all. King David's grave can be seen in the old churchyard in Heptonstall.

Leave the station car park in Mytholmroyd and turn left under the railway arches to head up the B6138 Cragg Road for 300m. At the pottery and craft shop (the former village fire station), turn right up Stocks Lane, then left on Nest Lane. A further 200m on, a fingerpost on the left indicates the path to Daisy Bank and Erringden Moor.

INFORMATION

Distance: 9 km (5.5 miles).

Start and finish: Mytholmroyd Railway Station.

Terrain: This is a varied walk which includes some remote moorland. Boots and a waterproof are essential.

Public transport: Mytholmroyd is well served by buses and trains from Rochdale, Burnley and Halifax.

Refreshments: Mytholmroyd has a tea shop, two fish & chip shops and a handful of pubs including the Dusty Miller, where the coiners regularly met, and the Shoulder of Mutton.

Looking towards Cragg Vale and Great Manshead from Erringden Moor, above Broadhead Clough.

The steep track narrows into a fenced path after about 500m and passes through a small plantation. At the top of the hill a stile on the left puts you in a short walled track. At the end, climb another stile and bear right, past a small cairn, to the edge of Broadhead Clough. Spring Wood, which carpets the floor and sides of Broadhead Clough, is managed as a nature reserve.

The path hugs the wall for 400m to a corner where a waymarker post directs you a short distance across Erringden Moor to a wooden fingerpost. Bear left here, back towards the clough, along a long-crumbled wall and ditch. This is the right of way; most locals stick to the clough edge, and the RoW is hard to discern and boggy in places. Both routes meet again at a marker pole.

Keep to the worn path, exceptionally wet in places, round the clough head. There it veers away from the clough for a short distance before, in the middle of the swamp, a right of way bears left, towards the small farmstead of Bell House. This path does not exist on the ground; it is more convenient to keep on to the gravel drive, which cuts down to the farm a little further on.

Bell House, once home to 'King' David Hartley, leader of the Cragg Vale Coiners.

From the house, bear right along the wallside to cross a small, boggy stream to a stile. Over that, follow the sunken path ahead for 500m to climb another stile near a metal shed, and descend the track to a third stile. Turn right, down the track to Higher Cragg. Past the farm houses the path goes through a well-signed wicket gate on the right, down a wooded sunken lane.

After 100m, by a small stone water channel, take a stile on the right and follow an old field hedge to climb the stile in the bottom left corner. A large water pipe guides you down towards a marker post, which directs you below Whams Wood into an old lane. Cross the stile at the end into a birch wood. You descend, past the bungalow at Spa Laithe Farm, to hit tarmac at Spa Bridge – a nearby spring was once thought by locals to have curative properties. It was also near here that Matthew Normanton, one of the coiners, was arrested. Before his execution he confessed to his part in the murder of William Deighton.

Cross Spa Bridge and head up to the B6138. Turn right for 100m, cross the road and take the path signed to Holderness Wood, which climbs between the two rows of cottages: Mid Birks and Twist Clough. Past Upper Birks, turn left towards the wood, passing through a red gate, then sharp right, up to another red gate. Only 10m through this bear left, across the field to a waymarked stile into the wood, beneath Robin Hood Rocks. The obvious path soon climbs to the wood top where a bench, near an old millstone, offers a welcome break and the best view of the day, of the Cragg Valley,

Mill stone in the woods above Cragg Vale.

Broadhead Clough and Erringden Moor, and down the Calder Valley towards Hebden Bridge, Heptonstall and Heptonstall Moor.

The path runs along the top of the wood for 1km, then climbs a stile which puts you on a track which descends gradually, through the wood edge, towards a stone shed and an electricity pole. Turn left past the shed, down the field and through a gate, to pass in front of the cottages at Hollin Hey. Turn right, along the track, which soon joins another coming from the left to meet Hall Bank Lane, which carries you back down to Mytholmroyd.

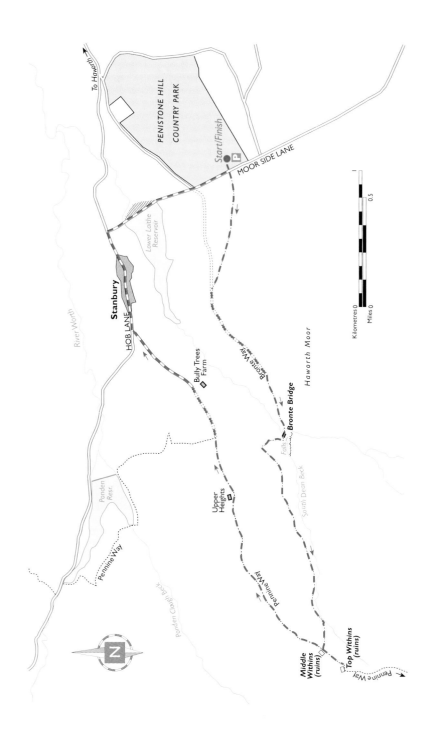

THE BRONTË MOORS

I f only, in the mid-19th century, someone had sold shares in the Brontë sisters. You only have to walk down Haworth main street to realise that sales from merchandise alone, never mind from poetry, novels and film rights, would have made anyone with a penny share a millionaire.

Emily, Anne and Charlotte were actually born near Bradford, and moved to Haworth with their father, Patrick Brontë (born Patrick Brunty in Northern Ireland), shortly after Anne's birth in 1820. Who knows what they would think of today's Brontë tea towels, gaudy paintings of Top Withins, Brontë biscuits and drinks.

What inspired the sisters wasn't the cobbled Main Street, the gift shoppes or the old weavers' cottages in the village, but the beautiful, wild moorland expanses beyond. Most visitors start this popular walk from Haworth itself but I prefer to start away from the crowds, at nearby Penistone Hill Country Park. The walk, which would have been very familiar to the young Brontë sisters, is best done midweek, when the moors are quiet and you have the stunning scenery and the song of the curlew to yourself.

From the lower of the two car park entrances off Moor Side Lane cross the road and follow the path indicated by a metal fingerpost to a kissing gate.

INFORMATION

Distance: 10 km (6.25 miles).

Start and finish: Car park on the west side of Penistone Hill Country Park, off Moor Side Lane, near Haworth.

Terrain: Well-used and signed moorland paths and tracks. Though most of the route is well-signed, people still manage to get lost on the moors, particularly during poor visibility. Top Withins is in an exposed position and waterproofs should be carried. Boots recommended.

Public transport: Buses to Haworth run from Bradford Interchange. The nearest mainline rail station is Keighley, and steam trains from there run to Haworth along the Worth Valley Railway line. For steam train details contact 01535 645214. A summer Sunday minibus service from Haworth passes Penistone Hill; services from Bradford stop near Lower Laithe Reservoir on their way to Stanbury.

Continued on next page.

The view across the valley to Stanbury.

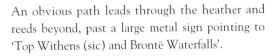

Refreshments:
Stanbury has pubs, and you might encounter ice cream or snack vans at Penistone Hill. Nearby Haworth has restaurants, teashop and pubs.

Opening hours:
Brontë Parsonage Museum, Haworth, Keighley BD22 8DR (01535 642323) is open Apr-Sep 1000-1700, Oct-Mar 1100-1630.

An obvious path leads through the heather and reeds beyond, past a large metal sign pointing to 'Top Withens (sic) and Brontë Waterfalls'.

The path drops to a dusty vehicle track which carries you along the contour for 1.3km to a flight of stone steps down to Brontë Bridge. The falls are reached by a rough path up the side of the clough on your left, as you cross a small flag bridge over its waters. The falls are pretty but unremarkable, resembling many other falls encountered in the cloughs that drain the extensive moors in the South Pennines.

Today's Brontë Bridge, a simple stone affair crossing South Dean Beck, is not as the Brontë family would remember it. A flashflood on 19 May 1989 swept away the old bridge, and it was replaced a year later.

Brontë Bridge on Haworth Moor.

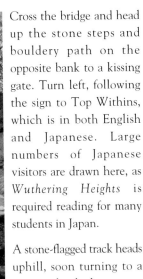

Cross the bridge and head up the stone steps and bouldery path on the opposite bank to a kissing gate. Turn left, following the sign to Top Withins, which is in both English and Japanese. Large numbers of Japanese visitors are drawn here, as *Wuthering Heights* is required reading for many students in Japan.

A stone-flagged track heads uphill, soon turning to a worn path which contours through fields, past several ruined farms, eventually rising to the ruins of Middle Withins Farm, from where the flagged Pennine Way leads you left, up to the ruins of Top Withins.

This was supposedly the inspiration for Emily's *Wuthering Heights* but while the setting seems right, the building itself would have been far too modest to be compared with the sizeable house described in the novel, which is more likely to have been based on Shibden Hall, near Halifax.

TOP WITHENS.
THIS FARMHOUSE HAS BEEN ASSOCIATED WITH
"WUTHERING HEIGHTS"
THE EARNSHAW HOME IN EMILY BRONTË'S
NOVEL.
THE BUILDINGS, EVEN WHEN COMPLETE, BORE
NO RESEMBLANCE TO THE HOUSE SHE
DESCRIBED,
BUT THE SITUATION MAY HAVE BEEN IN HER
MIND WHEN SHE WROTE OF THE MOORLAND
SETTING OF THE HEIGHTS.

BRONTË SOCIETY   THIS PLAQUE HAS BEEN PLACED HERE
1964   IN RESPONSE TO MANY INQUIRIES.

Brontë Society plaque on Top Withins, inspiration for Emily Brontë's *Wuthering Heights*.

Some Pennine Way guides refer to there being a bothy at Top Withins but signs there warn that the ruins are dangerous and advise against entering. The only creatures to feel at home here are the semi-tame sheep that gather around the ruins in the hope of scrounging scraps from the many visitors. Some get quite brave and are not afraid of raiding rucksacks while owners are distracted by the surrounding moors.

Head back down the Pennine Way flags for 2km to a white painted Pennine farmhouse – Upper Heights Cottage – to turn left, following the sign for the Pennine Way and Stanbury. In another 500m, ignore the junction of paths, where the Pennine Way turns left to Ponden Reservoir, and keep on for Stanbury, over the cattle grid 300m down the track at Bully Trees Farm. From here the lane leads down to Hob Lane, just outside Stanbury. Turn right to enter the village, past Stanbury First School and the small church, built in 1848, on the left, just before the Friendly Inn and the old village co-op.

Pass through the village and take the first road on the right, signed for Oxenhope. The road carries you over the dam wall of Lower Laithe Reservoir before climbing back up to Penistone Hill in just under 1km.

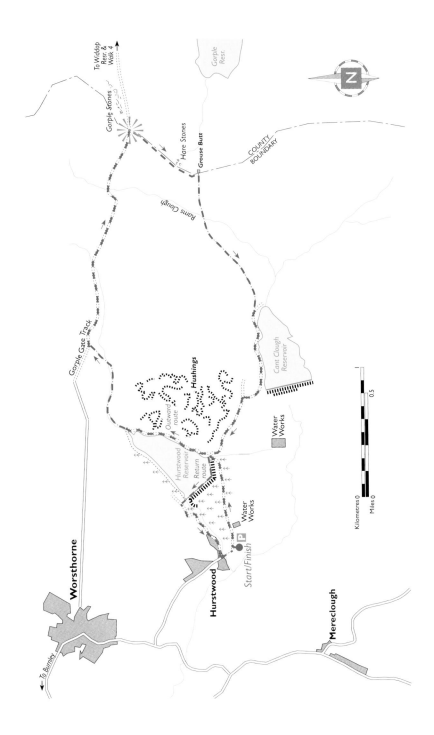

HURSTWOOD

Before the Industrial Revolution changed the face of transportation with the development of the canal and rail networks, South Pennine farmers faced a problem when they wanted lime to sweeten their agricultural land or for use in mortar, necessary for construction. They had the choice of carrying it long distances by packhorse from the Yorkshire Dales, or looking closer to home for a source.

At Hurstwood and a few other places in the district they found what they were looking for, buried under layers of clay, sand and soil. In the 17th and 18th centuries those who exploited the limestone found a simple but effective method of extracting it, called 'hushing'. They dug a complex of small canals in the hillside above the buried limestone boulders, to drain water from the moors into dammed ponds. It was then let out in a torrent, swilling away the topsoil to reveal the limestone beneath.

The completion of the Leeds-Liverpool Canal in 1816 helped bring an end to the need for hushings as lime could now be easily and cheaply transported from elsewhere. This figure-of-eight walk climbs from Hurstwood Reservoir to the Pennine watershed on the Yorkshire/ Lancashire border, via the worked landscape between Cant Clough Reservoir and Smallshaw Clough.

INFORMATION

Distance: 9 km (5.5 miles).

Start and finish: Picnic site car park, Hurstwood.

Terrain: Moorland and reservoir-edge. Boots and waterproofs recommended.

Refreshments: None on route.

Public transport: No bus service - minibuses from Burnley stop at Worsthorne, just over a kilometre away.

Hurstwood Hall in Hurstwood village.

From the car park at Hurstwood head through the kissing gate in the top left corner. Turn right up the track, past the conifer woods on the left. On the moors beyond you'll see the whirring blades of Coal Clough wind power station.

The steep, grassy bank of the reservoir soon appears on your left; ignore the footpath sign at the top end of the dam and stick to the track, which carries you over a channel carrying water into the dam from Cant Clough and along the water's edge past a large area of 'sheddings' – piles of gritstone discarded as the extracted lime was fired in kilns nearby. At the end of the reservoir, where Hurstwood Brook enters the dam, ignore the footbridge on the left and the apparent left fork in the track, to veer right along a ruined wall by the stream. Take care not to stray into the hushings – you might never be seen again!

Spoil heaps, remains of the hushings around Hurstwood reservoir.

Stick to the stream side and, after only a few hundred metres, find the ruined stone walls of an oval sheep fold. Leave the brook and bear ahead left past the fold; a very faint path curves gently up the hill to turn right on the Gorple Track, an old packhorse route between Worsthorne and Heptonstall.

The track climbs, across Rams Clough, to the watershed which marks the boundary between Yorkshire and Lancashire, just below Gorple Stones. The view from here is very fine indeed – Gorple Reservoir and Heptonstall Moor ahead, boggy Black Hameldon hill to your right, and Cant Clough Reservoir behind. In summer the area is alive with bird song – larks, pipits, grouse, golden plover, curlew and even Canada geese on Gorple Reservoir all contribute to the symphony.

At the boundary sign bear right, along the marshy watershed to the chunky Hare Stones just 300m away, a pile of weathered gritstone boulders which provide a sheltered spot for a snack before you continue along the watershed for a further 100m, to a collapsed grouse butt. Here, at a point indicated by a small cairn, a path takes you right, down into Rams Clough and over the stream to climb left up the opposite bank on to the well-waymarked permissive bridleway which drops towards Cant Clough Reservoir.

Follow the reservoir-side track right; it passes through the stone wall on your right after 300m. When you are parallel with the dam wall, turn right up a concrete track, back towards Hurstwood Reservoir. There you cross your outward route to pass through a kissing gate on to the path along the dam wall to the end, where a metal footbridge on your left brings you into a pine plantation. Ahead, through the trees, a wooden stile brings you on to the Burnley Way down which you turn left, to a kissing gate, following an obvious track beyond through a field to a wooden stile. Beyond this a lane carries you back into Hurstwood.

Edmund Spenser, poet and author of *The Faerie Queen*, lived in Spenser House in the village for two years from 1576 and fell for local beauty Rose Dyneley. She spurned his approaches but still got a name check – as "fair Roselynd" – in his *Shepherd's Calendar*. To return to the car park turn left at the red phone box, just beyond Hurstwood Church.

Spenser House, Hurstwood, once home to the poet Edmund Spenser.

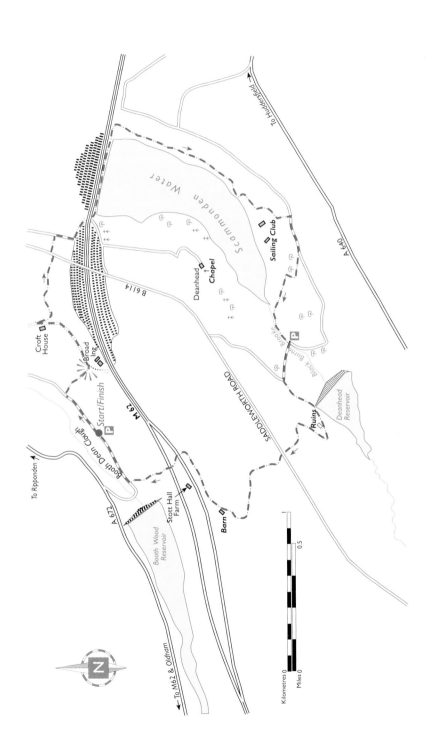

SCAMMONDEN WATER AND THE M62

Scammonden Water was one of the last Pennine reservoirs to be built, and is perhaps the most spectacular, having as its enormous north-facing wall nothing less than the M62 motorway. Yet despite the heavy roar of the trans-Pennine traffic it is possible to admire this great feat of engineering and then escape, along the peaceful water's edge, on to the moors beyond.

Sails on Scammonden Reservoir.

INFORMATION

Distance: 9 km (5.5 miles).

Start and finish: Car park near Booth Wood Reservoir above Dean Clough, 5km from Ripponden on the A672 Oldham Road.

Terrain: Very varied, from wooded cloughs to open moor and reservoir edge. Boots and waterproofs recommended.

Refreshments: None on route.

Public transport: Bus services between Halifax and Oldham stop near Booth Wood Reservoir.

Leaving the car park, head away from the reservoir; 400m along Moselden Lane, turn right over a rickety stile at the top of a short flight of stone steps. The path beyond carries you along the line of an old wall, kinking slightly right half way up, to continue along a fence to the farm buildings at Broad Ing. As you approach the stile in the top corner, stick to the fence on the firmer ground. Climb the stile and turn left along the track. On your left is a wonderful hill panorama.

You can stride out easily along the firm track which carries you past Croft House. Just beyond, by the first telegraph pole on the left, a path doubles back to the right taking you up to a footbridge across Moss Moor Catchwater Drain.

Bearing slightly left, uphill from the bridge, the path leads over rough pasture to a stile; over this bear right, in the opposite direction to that indicated by a fingerpost, through an area of recently planted trees. As you crest the hill you have your first view of Scammonden Water. Built by Huddersfield Corporation to take advantage of an annual 130 cm of rainfall, engineers formed a unique union with the motorway authorities to construct an embankment which not only held back the dam's waters but also carried the M62. Car parks, picnic areas and various paths were created, and the area was declared open by the Queen in 1971.

The path leads down through a car park to the B6114, along which you turn left for 50 m and cross the road to head down the grassy lane opposite, to Scammonden Road. Turning right, to the end of the road, you'll find a stile on the left. A surfaced track carries you down to the side of the M62 and beneath it in a tunnel.

Through that turn left, along the narrow dam-wall path, then turn right, past the plaque marking the opening of the dam. A track carries you parallel to the water until a sign diverts you around the sailing club, up a narrow path. At the top bear right, to follow the Kirklees Way to the southern end of Scammonden dam. Beyond the main body of water, ignore two footbridges over Black Burne Brook on your right, and follow the brook to a small car park in New Lane.

Looking across Dean Head Reservoir to Dean Head Moor.

Turn right, up New Lane, which offers good views back over the dam. At a sharp right bend, turn left on to the dirt track to Dean Head Reservoir. You abandon the Kirklees Way by the dam wall, climbing the concrete-topped wall corner carefully – there is no proper stile. Walk up the field ahead, with the wall on your right, past the ruins of what must once have been a substantial farmhouse.

Keep on to the next ruined farm, just above which the track doglegs right into a sunken lane. At the top it levels out. Climb the stile here and follow the sunken path diagonally across the next field to cross a large wooden stile. Maintain your direction for a further 50m, through a levelled wall, to veer right to Saddleworth Road.

The view from the ruined farm, across Dean Head Reservoir to Black Heath.

Your path continues across the road, following a sunken, boggy track over the brow and downhill, soon swinging right through an old gateway, down to a neatly walled lane and past the barn at High Moss. An ornately carved ram's head is set above the barn door, a reminder of the industry which spawned this area's greatest wealth.

The track soon passes under the west-bound carriageway of the M62. Stranded in the middle of the motorway, on your left, is Stott Hall Farm – life here must be very noisy. The track continues under the east-bound lanes where your route now runs off the track, straight down the fenceside ahead, crossing the track again to drop through a small plantation by a small marker post. Don't follow the track – the gate at the end is usually locked. At the foot of the plantation turn right, up Moselden Lane, to return to the car park.

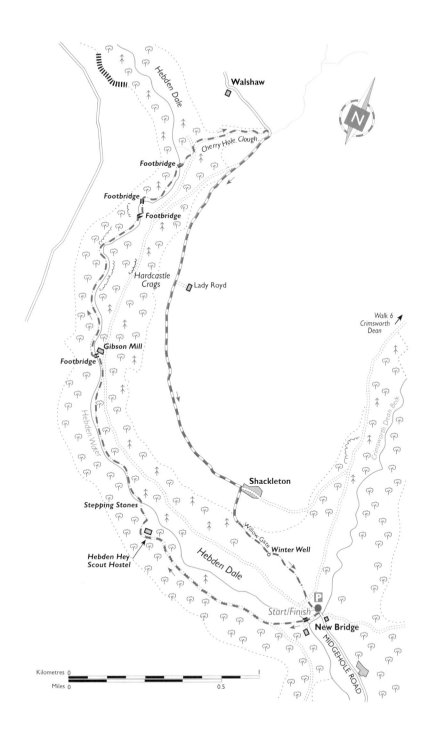

Walshaw

Hebden Dale

Cherry Hole Clough

Footbridge

Footbridge

Footbridge

Hardcastle Crags

Lady Royd

Walk 6
Crimsworth Dean

Gibson Mill

Footbridge

Hebden Water

Crimsworth Dean Beck

Shackleton

Stepping Stones

Hebden Hey
Scout Hostel

Hebden Dale

Willow Gate   Winter Well

Start/Finish

New Bridge

MIDGEHOLE ROAD

Kilometres 0 — 1
Miles 0 — 0.5

HARDCASTLE CRAGS AND GIBSON MILL

INFORMATION

Distance: 8 km (5 miles).

Start and finish: National Trust car park, Midgehole Road, Hebden Bridge.

Terrain: Most of this walk is on firm tracks and paths, though there might be some mud after rain. Boots recommended.

Public transport: Mini-bus services from Hebden Bridge serve Hardcastle Crags every day except Sunday.

Refreshments: A snack van, offering such treats as baked potatoes and soup as well as drinks, cakes and sandwiches, operates at Gibson Mill most weekends and other busy days. The 'Blue Pig' working men's club at Midgehole is often open to walkers.

Note: The National Trust charges for parking. An honesty system operates when the car park is unattended. Trail leaflets, describing waymarked routes through the property, are on sale at the information caravan.

Hardcastle Crags is a natural jewel at the heart of the South Pennines. The wooded valley, through which Hebden Water tumbles along a rocky river bed, is home to a rich diversity of birdlife – including dippers, fly-catchers, green woodpeckers and birds of prey – and flora including vast swathes of bluebells in spring, rare ferns and scented wild garlic.

From the lower car park, walk back through the Lodge gates and turn right to cross Hebden Water on New Bridge. It's hard to believe that a large mill once stood here which, like Gibson Mill, enjoyed a brief life as a cafe entertaining the hundreds of visitors who flocked here at the turn of the last century.

The old kitchen in Gibson Mill.

Over the bridge, directly ahead, a track leads up to the right, past a house called Cairn Acre, and narrows to meet, after 100m, a surfaced track. Turn right, to Hebden Hey Scout Hostel. On the way you will pass Hawden Hall, formerly Hawden Hole. Before the barn was converted into the luxurious dwelling it is now, a small cottage stood at the side of the track and it was here, in 1817, that two men broke in and strangled an old weaver, Sammy o'Kattys. Among their haul was an unsigned pound note and when one of the pair tried to buy goods with it in Hebden Bridge they were arrested for the murder, tried and hanged. Billy Holt, mentioned in Walk 23, ran a holiday camp here in 1919.

The next building you come to is Hebden Hey Scout Hostel – the path is well waymarked through the hostel yard. According to local legend, in a cave nearby lived Tom Bell, a rogue who would leave his cave after dark, armed with a sword and clad in chain mail, to raid local homes. He wore the soles of his shoes back to front to deceive pursuers. A stone head, said to depict his face, is set into the wall above one of the hostel doors.

Gibson Mill, a relic of the Industrial Revolution at the heart of Hardcastle Crags.

Pass in front of the hostel buildings to a very old causey path which heads down to a line of stepping stones across Hebden Water at Cosy Corner. Follow the path on the opposite bank, upstream, to Gibson Mill. This valley has long been popular with walkers and Gibson Mill, a cotton mill dating from 1800, became something of a pleasure park when production ceased at the end of the last century, with swing boats, stables, cafes and a 500-seat restaurant. Today the mill is much quieter, though the National Trust has plans for a small cafe, information facilities and toilets.

Cross the river by the bridge next to the mill and follow the path right, past two old mill ponds, to hug the riverbank for 800m, crossing three wooden footbridges. Having crossed the last, head away from the river to a junction of dirt tracks by a small stone bridge. Turn left over the bridge, then up, through a gap in the wall on the right, into Cherry Hole Clough. Follow the slippery path uphill, watching out for wood ant nests. The clough hides an enchanting waterfall and was at one time reputedly laid out formally with footbridges and flowering rhododendrons.

At the top of the clough turn right along the track which serves the farms above the Crags. At the only junction, your way left is clearly signed 'Hardcastle Crags via Shackleton'. The track gives open views down the Hebden Valley. One of the farms passed, Ladyroyd, was until the 1950s a school house, serving local youngsters. A row of coat hooks can still be seen on the wall in one of the barns.

After another 1.5km, before the cluster of cottages and barns that form the hamlet of Shackleton, turn right, through a steel field gate, and, at a redundant stone gatepost, turn left down a walled path. Turning left over the stile at the bottom, take the left fork at the junction just ahead, past the huge boulder known as Slurring Rock; grooves in the rock were worn by youngsters whose favourite game years ago was to slide – or slurr – down the angled boulder on their clog irons - almost an early form of roller-blading!

Slurring Rock, down which youngsters slid on their clog irons.

Follow the paved path ahead, the old packhorse way known as Willow Gate, past the site of Winter Well at the bottom of the woodland, where livestock would have been brought to water during cold winters or dry summers, as it was said the waters there never dried up – as if to prove the point a small row of stepping stones help you cross the mud, so that you arrive back at the car park just ahead with dry feet.

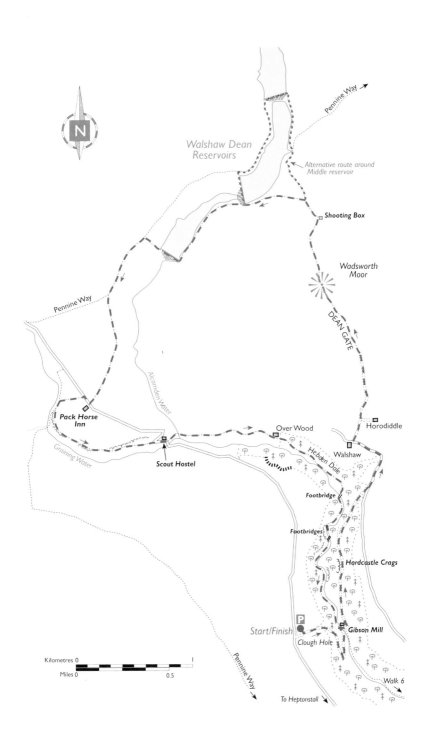

N

Walshaw Dean
Reservoirs

Pennine Way

Alternative route around
Middle reservoir

Shooting Box

Wadsworth
Moor

Pennine Way

DEAN GATE

Alcomden Water

Pack Horse
Inn

Over Wood

Horodiddle

Hebden Dale

Walshaw

Graining Water

Scout Hostel

Footbridge

Footbridges

Hardcastle Crags

Start/Finish

Gibson Mill

Clough Hole

Walk 6

Kilometres 0   1
Miles 0   0.5

Pennine Way

To Heptonstall

WALSHAW DEAN

The Hardcastle Crags valley, explored in Walk 16, draws ramblers from across the north of England. At weekends and on Bank Holidays hundreds walk the woodland paths between Midgehole and Gibson Mill. But few venture further upstream, where the valley is just as beautiful yet far quieter, and paths lead across the moors to a scenic chain of upland reservoirs.

From the car park at Clough Hole, a rough Land Rover track winds down through beech woods to cross Hebden Water into Gibson Mill's yard. Past the mill cottages, turn left up the main valley track, past the gritstone outcrops after which the area is named. 'Hardcastle Crags' may be derived from the elements 'hardt' (towering), 'cas' (steep) and 'craig' (rock).

One of the crags in the Hebden Valley after which the Hardcastle Crags estate was named.

Continue uphill, ignoring a fork in the track, climbing out of the woods to a T-junction at which you turn left to Walshaw, the impressive shooting seat of Lord Savile. Just as you enter Walshaw's yard turn right, up the side of a cottage along a lane past the drive to Horrodiddle cottage. A permissive path on your right, signed 'Walshaw Dean', climbs a small bank to a field gate through which you turn left, on a grassy track, then left again into a walled lane past a plantation.

INFORMATION

Distance: 16 km (10 miles).

Start and finish: Clough Hole car park, 3km beyond Heptonstall on Widdop Road, above Hebden Bridge.

Terrain: Woodland paths and open moor. Boots and waterproofs recommended.

Public transport: Bus service to Widdop Gate from Hebden Bridge on Summer Sundays stop at Clough Hole on request; services to Slack run throughout the year except on Sundays.

Refreshments: A friendly snack van operates at Gibson Mill at weekends, bank holidays and during the summer. The Pack Horse Inn, known locally as the Ridge, is about three-quarters of the way through the walk. *Notes:* Paths between Walshaw and the Pennine Way are mostly permissive routes, by permission of Savile Estates and Yorkshire Water, and as such can be closed during the grouse season (12 August to 10 December) or when major engineering work is

Continued on next page.

being carried out on the reservoirs. If uncertain, contact Calderdale Countryside Service (01422 359454). At the time of writing the path around Middle Walshaw Dean Reservoir was closed and the Pennine Way subject to a well-signed diversion, but these paths were due to re-open before publication.

At the other end, your way is indicated by a Savile Estates sign, pointing ahead on to Wadsworth Moor. The initial path is narrow but the greater part has been made up to take Land Rovers and offers an excellent panorama of the surrounding moors and reservoirs. Ahead, below appropriately-named Heather Hill, you can see the patchwork pattern created by burning heather, to improve the habitat for grouse and other birds. Grouse feed on young heather shoots but need deeper heather as cover from the elements and predators. Careful, regular burning by the gamekeepers provides the necessary variety.

As you drop to a small shooting box – a good lunch stop as there's a round stone table outside – a view of the Walshaw Dean reservoirs opens up. Work on the dams began in 1900 and a shanty town, nicknamed Dawson City, was built near Heptonstall to accommodate the labourers. On completion two of the dams were found to leak and they did not go on-stream until 1915.

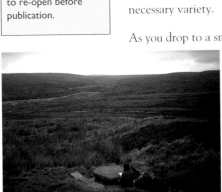

The round table outside the shooting hut above Walshaw Dean.

From the shooting box continue downhill. At a fork you have a choice. The rougher path, right, takes you down to the dams for a well-signed anti-clockwise circuit of the middle reservoir, completed by following the Pennine Way back across the middle dam to this bank.

The left fork offers a shorter route, dropping past a brick gamekeeper's store to pass through a green gate – if this is locked climb the step stile on the right. Here the two options meet again to follow the path along the south side of the lower dam. At the time of writing, this permissive path carried the Pennine Way, diverted during engineering work on the reservoirs. Canada geese and barnacle geese can often be seen on the reservoir or grazing in the fields alongside.

A metal footbridge carries the path on to the dam wall, beyond which, on a recently tarred track, you turn left for 600m to a fork. Bear left to a wooden step stile, over which you aim for a marker post in the field ahead. This directs you ahead left to another stile, then right, over two more fields, to the Pack Horse Inn which has a display of material about the reservoir.

Those not tempted by the pub should turn right along Widdop Road for 75m, then over a ladder stile on the left. The path drops to a stile; turn left, not on the flagged Pennine Way down to Graining Water, but the higher path, along the top edge of the clough where you might see wheatear, or even a short-eared owl. The path contours along the clough edge before descending to a wall corner, beyond which a kissing gate brings you to Blake Dean.

Heather moors surround Walshaw Dean's upper and middle reservoirs.

Turn right, down the road to pass through a wicket gate on your left, just before the bridge. Steps lead down to the side of Graining Water which joins Alcomden Water here to form Hebden Water. Cross the footbridge and bear right, up stone steps.

Near the top of the bank a broad grassy path, part of the line of the former railway, forks right. This leads you over a wooden step stile, narrows as it enters the Scots pine wood, then passes Over Wood cottage, where it joins a firm track.

A kilometre beyond the cottage, just over a small stone bridge, the track forks; bear right, over Hebden Water. Follow the river downstream, over two more footbridges, back to Gibson Mill. Instead of crossing into the mill yard, retrace your earlier route back up to the car park.

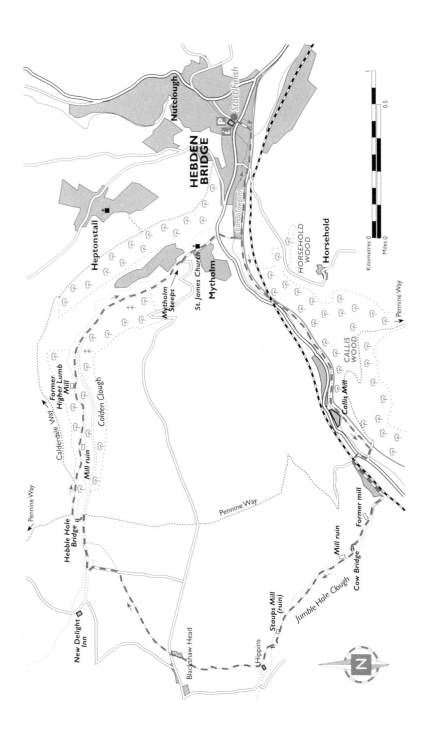

JUMBLE HOLE CLOUGH

In the early days of the Industrial Revolution, before steam power led to the growth of valley-bottom mill towns to which coal could easily be transported by canal or rail, many small South Pennine cloughs were home to a surprising number of small, water-powered mills.

Jumble Hole Clough was one such – in the 18th and 19th centuries four mills exploited the stream that tumbles down the rocky clough bottom. The mills were built in the cloughs rather than along the banks of the larger River Calder as it was the fall of water that counted, rather than the volume. Whereas the Calder fell only 5 metres per km between Todmorden and Sowerby Bridge, tributary streams fell by an average of 55m, making it easier to gain a head of water to drive the waterwheels.

Today Jumble Hole's mills are romantic ruins slowly being reclaimed by nature, and the valley is a peaceful haven which will delight walkers.

From Hebden Bridge Tourist Information Centre cross into Holme Street, which leads to the Rochdale Canal towpath. Turn right, past Hebble End Mill craft centre. Beyond the Stubbing Wharf canalside pub is Rawden Mill Lock, where you'll often find wooden canal lock gates piled high – Callis Mill, on your right, is the head-quarters for the canal restoration project.

Just before the next bridge, turn right through the fence, past a Pennine Way board, to cross the A646. Turn right for 200m to Underbank Avenue. Under the railway arch turn left, past several houses, then turn right, up Jumble Hole Road.

Underbank carding mill is the first of the old mills you'll pass. The overgrown ruins of the second, Spa Mill, on both sides of the track are just a little further up; the large wall on the right was a retaining wall for its storage reservoir.

INFORMATION

Distance: 10 km (6.25 miles).

Start and finish: Tourist Information Centre, Hebden Bridge.

Terrain: Wooded valleys, meadows and canal towpath.

Public transport: Hebden Bridge is well served by trains from the York-Blackpool coast to coast service, and local services from Leeds, Bradford, Littleborough and Manchester Piccadilly. Buses from Halifax, Rochdale, Burnley and Keighley.

Refreshments: Hebden Bridge has restaurants and teashops, a good curry house and several pubs. The New Delight at Jack Bridge, Colden, is halfway along the walk, just a few hundred metres off-route.

Note: Waymarks and fingerposts in the Blackshawhead area are frequently vandalised. Pay careful attention to the directions and the map.

Where the track sweeps right you bear left, to Cowbridge, site of the third mill. Just upstream, off the path, is an enchanting series of small waterfalls. Cross the stream on Cow Bridge. The switchback track heads up the wooded clough, past Cowbridge's mill pond and through a gate, ignoring paths on the left and right. Increasingly narrow, the path climbs higher above the rocky gorge.

You soon reach the haunting ruin of Staups Mill, once a four-storey cotton spinning mill with an 8m diameter water wheel which stood in a pit against the mill wall. It is best left unexplored as the remaining walls are no longer secure.

Upstream from the mill, cross the footbridge and climb the steps opposite to bear left at a fingerpost, in the direction of Hippins. Go through the wicket gate at the side of this 17th century house whose name means 'stepping stones'.

Top: Weirs above Cow Bridge in Jumble Hole Clough.

Bottom: The clapper bridge at Hebble Hole, over Colden Water.

Head up the track signed 'Lower Blackshaw Head' and pass through a stile at the side of a huge stone barn, then up a field edge path to cross Apple Tree Farm's drive. Through a Calderdale Way-marked gap stile, a flagged path carries you over two stiles, after which you bear left for a few metres, then right, to a kissing gate and a step stile beyond.

Turn left up a track to the Blackshaw Head road. Cross and follow the well-signed Calderdale Way through meadows and stiles; a yellow wicket gate delivers you into a rocky walled lane, down which you drop to Shaw Bottom cottage. Turn left down the tarmac for 50 metres.

The skeletal ruins of Staups Mill.

The thirsty or hungry can bear left for 400m to the New Delight, returning here afterwards. Otherwise, turn right for 400m, to a path that drops left, down steps, into Colden Clough where you will find ancient Hebble Hole bridge, built from four huge stone slabs. Once it would have carried pack ponies on their way to the Cloth Hall at Heptonstall – today it carries the Pennine Way, the Calderdale Way and yourself over Colden Water. Follow the causey path right, along the wood top. Where it forks, by a stone step stile in the wall ahead, bear right, down among the trees.

Past an overgrown quarry you soon come to a wide bend in a track which you follow down to the streamside, past old mill ponds and weirs. Beyond these bear right again, past a solitary mill chimney on the spot where Higher Lumb Mill once stood, crossing the culverted stream to a steel gate, near Lower Lumb Mill's chimney. Follow the track ahead for a kilometre; it ends on the steep tarmac road known as Mytholm Steeps.

Turn left, past St James' Church, down to the A646. Cross and pass through a gap in the wall opposite, to follow Colden Water on its way to the River Calder. Cross the river on a footbridge, and go up the side of Stubbing Square to turn left on the towpath, back to Hebden Bridge.

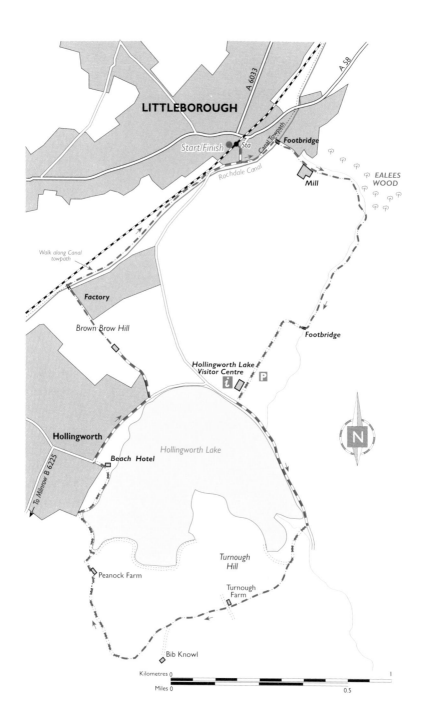

LITTLEBOROUGH

A 6033

A 58

Start/Finish   Sta   Footbridge

Canal Towpath

Rochdale Canal

Mill

EALEES
WOOD

Walk along Canal
towpath

Factory

Brown Brow Hill

Footbridge

Hollingworth Lake
Visitor Centre

P

Hollingworth

To Milnrow B 6225

Hollingworth Lake

Beach Hotel

N

Turnough
Hill

Peanock Farm

Turnough
Farm

Bib Knowl

Kilometres 0   1

Miles 0   0.5

HOLLINGWORTH LAKE

The Rochdale Canal, opened in 1804, was the first of the trans-Pennine canals. Goods transported between Sowerby Bridge, in West Yorkshire, and Manchester, included wool and cotton, timber and coal. When the route was being surveyed in the 1760s, by the engineer James Brindley, it was realised that water would have to be artificially supplied to the canal, which climbed from either side of the Pennines to 200m above sea-level, otherwise constant use of the locks would soon leave it, literally, high and dry.

Several reservoirs were constructed to keep the waters flowing and Hollingworth Lake, opened in 1798, was one of the first. Its waters were pumped a short way uphill into a channel which flowed to Summit, between Littleborough and Todmorden, the canal's appropriately-named highest point. The lake became an increasingly popular visitor attraction known far and wide as the 'weavers' seaport'; hotels sprang up around the water's edge as crowds came to dance, sail, fish and swim – including Captain Matthew Webb, the first ever cross-Channel swimmer in 1875. Despite the closure of the canal in 1952, the lake has remained popular and Lake Bank, on the western shore, still resembles a seafront with fish and chip shops, ice cream parlours and amusement arcades.

The area was declared a country park in 1974 and nature reserves have been created on the quieter shores of the lake, which attract a wide variety of birdlife including

INFORMATION

Distance: 7.5 km (4.5 miles).

Start and finish: George Stephenson Square, Littleborough Railway Station.

Terrain: An easy walk with little noticeable ascent, though some parts can be muddy, so boots are recommended.

Public transport: Littleborough can be reached by bus or train from Rochdale or Halifax, Burnley and Todmorden.

Refreshments: Cafes and pubs a-plenty in Littleborough and around Hollingworth Lake; in Hollingworth itself you can buy everything from candy floss to fish and chips.

Opening hours: Hollingworth Lake Vistor Centre has displays of local history and wildlife, including a hoard of Roman coins found nearby. Open Apr-October 1030-1900 Mon-Fri, 1030-2000 Sat-Sun (cafe 1100-1700). There is also a Heritage Centre in Lodge Street, Littleborough.

The Rochdale Canal at Littleborough.

snipe, little and great crested grebe, mute swans, reed bunting and tufted ducks.

From George Stephenson Square at Littleborough Railway Station, pass under the line through the subway and turn left down Hollingworth Road, to join the Rochdale Canal towpath by Canal Street Garage. Cross the footbridge at Littleborough Bottom Lock and go up the path behind the terraced homes in Oak Street. At the end follow Ealees Lane ahead, past Ealees Mill and Old Mill Cottage, a good example of a modest handloom weaver's cottage.

When the track forks stay right, on a clearly waymarked grassy path that follows the stream, to cross a footbridge. A flagged path beyond leads you through a picnic area and along a surfaced track to Hollingworth Lake Visitor Centre.

Past the centre turn left along the lakeside promenade and Rakewood Road, for 700m, then right, along the country park track. The area on the right is a nature reserve and while the sensitive area is out of bounds to the public, an information board provided by the Royal Society for the Protection of Birds details the wildlife you might see. To the left of that board, a waymarked path leads off the track, along boardwalk, to a kissing gate. Bear left through this, around Turnough Hill and, over a wooden stile, along the field edge to cross the lane in front of Turnough Farm, a long inhabited site, shown in deeds dating from 1274 as being home to one Garfride de Turnagh.

Looking back towards Bib Knowle, near Peanock Farm.

The obvious field edge path beyond leads to a kissing gate in the corner. Through this turn left on a rough track for 10 metres, then bear right on a

The view across Hollingworth Lake from Turnough.

path, dropping gently past a little quarry to another kissing gate. The obvious path beyond ignores a ladder stile to curve right, down to a farm track. Pass the cattle grid and continue on the lane for 500m to Peanock Farm. Its name is thought to derive from 'pinfold', small, walled enclosures in which stray livestock was held until its owners claimed it back. During the 1850s the farm was converted into a hotel to cater for the ever-increasing number of holidaymakers, but it has now reverted to a farm. Past the house turn right, under a stone arch, to the edge of Hollingworth Lake.

Turn left on the lakeside track for a few hundred metres; by the Beach Hotel you leave the lake for the fleshpots of Lake Bank. Bearing right along the main road, past the ice cream palours, chip shops and guesthouses, you'd be forgiven for thinking that you'd been mysteriously transported to some northern seaside resort.

At the far end of this 'golden quarter-mile' turn left down Heald Lane, through a steel gate and straight through the farmyard on Brown Brow Hill – sometimes very muddy after rain. Through another gate a field edge path, also muddy, carries you downhill past a factory to the canal bank. Since 1974 the Rochdale Canal Society has campaigned, with admirable success, for the re-opening of the canal and lengthy stretches are again open to boating traffic. Turn right along the towpath to return, after just over a kilometre, to Hollingworth Road and the railway station.

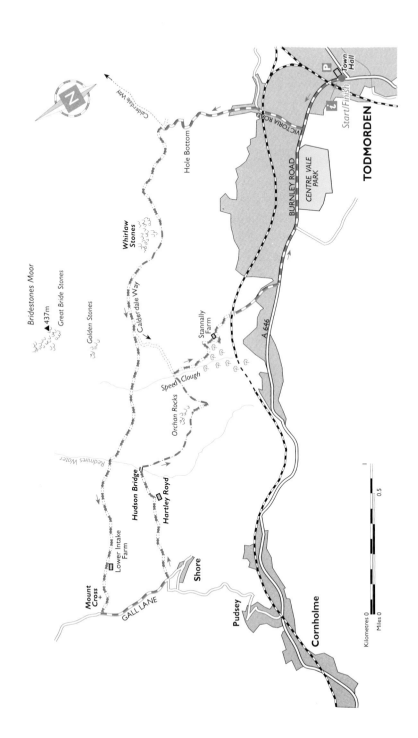

TODMORDEN

Start/Finish

Town Hall

P

VICTORIA ROAD

BURNLEY ROAD

CENTRE VALE PARK

A 646

Calderdale Way

Hole Bottom

Whirlaw Stones

Bridestones Moor

▲437m

Great Bride Stones

Golden Stones

Calderdale Way

Stannally Farm

Speed Clough

Orchan Rocks

Redmires Water

Hudson Bridge

Hartley Royd

Lower Intake Farm

Mount Cross

GALL LANE

Shore

Pudsey

Cornholme

Kilometres 0

Miles 0

0.5

WHIRLAW AND MOUNT CROSS

Exploring Whirlaw Stones.

The mysterious Whirlaw Stones rear above the town of Todmorden like an ancient burial mound. This heather-dotted outcrop of gritstone is a natural feature but it worked its magic on local author William Holt, whose novel *The Wizard of Whirlaw* tells the tale of a young weaver, Alan Haugh, taken under the wing of the reclusive philosopher William Heird, of Whirlaw. Heird's fiery adopted daughter Jane, who becomes Alan's lover, roams the stones at night, torching the heather to summon her swain from the valley bottom.

Man has also shaped the stones around Todmorden. Stone crosses and stoops were erected along the packhorse routes that criss-cross the hillsides and this walk passes Mount Cross, one of the finest in the area.

Start outside Todmorden's fine Town Hall, paid for by the Fielden family, who controlled a global trading business from Waterside Mills in the town. The Town Hall opened in 1875 and, until 1888, the Yorkshire/Lancashire boundary ran through its heart – the River Calder, which marked the boundary, flows under the hall.

Walk past the market, up Burnley Road, for 400m to turn right up Victoria Road. Just under the railway arch turn left up Meadow Bottom Road, past the Fountain Inn. Keep going up the steep hill into Hole Bottom Road, past Hole Bottom Mill chimney house. At the fork beyond go left, then

INFORMATION

Distance: 12km (7.5 miles).

Start and finish: Todmorden Town Hall. There is a large car park behind the Town Hall, off Halifax Road.

Terrain: Causey paths, packhorse routes and farm tracks. Some mud possible. Boots recommended.

Public transport: Todmorden is well served by buses and trains from Halifax, Rochdale and Burnley. Buses from Haworth and Keighley run to Todmorden during the summer.

Refreshments: Todmorden has a wide range of restaurants, inns, cafes and snack bars.

Opening hours: Todmorden's Tourist Information Centre in Burnley Road (01706 818181) frequently has displays of local paintings and photographs. Open Mon-Fri 900-1600, Sat 1000-1600, Sun 1100-1400.

right before the cottages at Ratcher, built beneath an imposing outcrop of gritstone. At a crossroad turn left along a bridleway and stay in this lane to Whirlaw Stones – there are fine views back across Todmorden through the tree canopy.

Before long Whirlaw looms large ahead. Keep ahead, to a step stile and lane gate, and continue on the lane beyond to another gate after which a superbly-preserved causey path leads to a walled lane which carries you beneath the wonderful gritstone outcrops on Bridestones Moor.

Where the lane forks, keep straight on, past a ruined house. After 2km the path goes around Lower Intake Farm and picks up the hard track just beyond. A short distance ahead on the right you'll notice Mount Cross. No-one is really sure about its origins. Some claim it marks the spot where the European missionary St Paulinus preached during the 7th century, while escorting Princess Ethelberga of Kent to Northumbria, to marry King Edwin. Others believe the cross might have been moved from the line of the Long Causeway, the medieval (or earlier) route which still carries traffic between Hebden Bridge and Burnley.

Hartley Royd, a superbly restored farmstead.

Continue to the end of the lane and turn left down Gall Lane for 700m, to turn left on a hairpin bend on to a bridleway, signed for Great Rock. On the right you can see roofless Shore Baptist Church and its graveyard. The lane carries you to the beautifully restored Hartley Royd, home in the 17th and 18th centuries to the forefathers of the Fieldens who built the Town Hall and many other impressive buildings in the area.

The impressive datestone on the house side is in Latin and, translated, reads JOHN FIELDEN AND WIFE ELIZABETH AT HOME FROM HARM 1724.

Turn left at the house through a stile by a five-bar gate, go 10m and over another stile, then along the grassy lane down to cross Redmires Water on Hudson's Bridge, part of a minor packhorse route that might have connected the Long Causeway with Lydgate in the valley bottom.

Cricket at Patmos, Todmorden.

Follow the path right, signed for Jumps Road. It soon becomes a lane which narrows to pass beneath fortress-like Orchan Rocks, down to a track on which you turn right, through a gate, then left down a wallside to a gap stile. Through this go left, up a farm driveway, then right through a wicket gate just before the house. The field side takes you to an iron gate in the corner. Cross Speed Clough and follow the fence ahead to a gate and stile.

Turn right and follow the Calderdale Way downhill past Stannally Farm. Under a huge railway tunnel turn left, down Stoney Royd Lane, to Burnley Road. Turn left to return to Todmorden. Just beyond Mons Mill you could cross the road to walk through Centre Vale Park, perhaps searching out the statue of John Fielden MP.

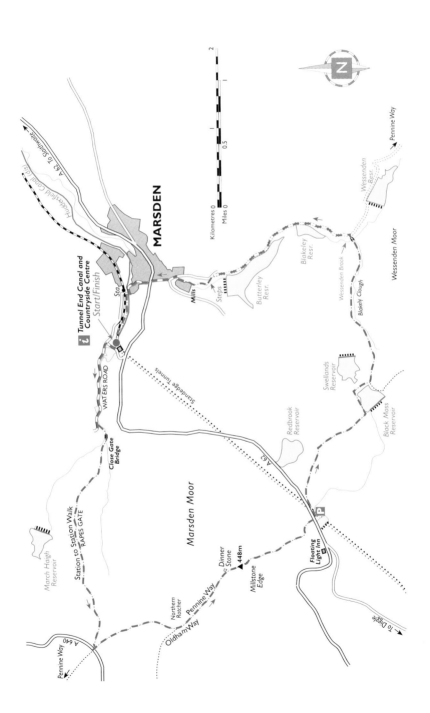

MARSDEN

Tunnel End Canal and
Countryside Centre
Start/Finish

Huddersfield Canal (dis)

A 62 To Slaithwaite

Sta.

Mills

Steps

Butterley Resr.

Blakeley Resr.

Wessenden Resr.

Pennine Way

Wessenden Brook

Wessenden Moor

Blakely Clough

Swellands Reservoir

Black Moss Reservoir

Redbrook Reservoir

Standedge Tunnels

WATERS ROAD

Close Gate Bridge

RAPES GATE

Station to Station Walk

March Haigh Reservoir

Marsden Moor

Dinner Stone

▲448m

Millstone Edge

Pennine Way

Northern Ratcher

Oldham Way

Pennine Way

A 640

A 62

Floating Light Inn

To Digle

Kilometres 0   0.5   2
Miles 0

MARSDEN MOOR

This superb excursion from Marsden, in the Colne Valley, traverses the most southerly of the moors featured in this book, actually crossing briefly from the South Pennines into the Peak National Park. It is, however, classic South Pennines landscape: atmospheric, lonely, reservoir-dotted moors crossed by packhorse routes, with a soundtrack provided by the bubbling of the curlew and the wavering song of the skylark. Two routes form much of our way: the old Rapes Highway, a packhorse route which linked the Colne Valley with Rochdale; and the modern Pennine Way, Britain's first National Trail, which opened in 1965. Other waymarked trails encountered on this route include the Standedge Way, Kirklees Way, Station to Station Walk and the Oldham Way, all providing an excellent means of discovering more about the area once the walks in this book have been tasted; details of some should be available at Tunnel End Centre, from where the walk begins.

Standedge Tunnel, which burrows into the hillside at Tunnel End, is the longest and highest canal tunnel in Britain. When the Huddersfield Narrow Canal was completed in 1774, boats arriving in Marsden from Huddersfield had to unload their cargoes which were then carried over the hills in carts, to be reloaded before completing the journey to Ashton-under-Lyme. Work on the first tunnel began in 1798 and it opened in 1811. Boats had to be 'legged' through – men lay on their backs and propelled the boats by pushing on the tunnel walls with their feet – the 6km journey taking four hours. The tunnel was locked in 1951 after the canal was abandoned but the Huddersfield Canal Society hopes to re-open it for leisure traffic.

From Tunnel End, walk back up to the Tunnel End Inn and turn left along Waters Road for a kilometre. About 100 metres past the Hey Green

INFORMATION

Distance: 17 km (10.5 miles).

Start and finish: Tunnel End Canal and Countryside Centre, Marsden.

Terrain: Open moor on which paths are mostly well-defined although navigation in poor weather might be difficult; in such circumstances map and compass must be carried.

Public transport: Marsden is served by buses from Huddersfield and Oldham daily, and Manchester on Saturdays. Trains from Huddersfield, Wakefield and Manchester stop in Marsden.

Refreshments: Often available at Tunnel End Canal and Countryside Centre (see below). Marsden has cafes, pubs and restaurants. The Floating Light public house (01457 874242) on Standedge, above Diggle, serves bar meals at lunch time and evenings all week during the summer, and on Thursday, Friday, Saturday and Sunday lunchtimes during the winter.

Continued on next page.

Hotel take the streamside path on the left, signed Willykay Clough, to cross Close Gate Bridge, a wonderfully preserved packhorse bridge, then turn right along an earth track. After 100m, ignoring a ford on the right, an old path swings left up the side of Stonepit Lee Clough. Easily identified, it traverses the moor to cross Willykay Clough, passing a succession of stone posts marked 'P H Road'. You are on Rapes Highway and the views behind are wonderful – in the Colne Valley is Marsden and beyond that Emley Moor TV transmitter; as you hop across Wilmer Green Clough the view back extends across the Dark Peak and Holme Moss.

Just before you reach the A640, a short section of stone flags brings you to a junction with the Pennine Way, down which you head, left, on a gravel surface built to cope with the pounding pressures of Pennine Wayfarers. This method of repair has largely been abandoned in favour of stone pitching, flags and raised mineral paths; it's easy to see why – its urban style has failed to blend into its wild environment.

At Northern Rotcher, where views of the Castleshaw dams open up before you, bear left past

Crossing Marsden Moor on Rape Gate, looking back to the Dark Peak.

a large cairn; the Pennine Way loses its gravelled surface again to follow the worn edge of a minor gritstone outcrop on the right. This section of the path is also utilised by the Oldham Way – you'll probably have noted the stone waymarker distinguishing the two, erected by the Pennine Way Association in 1996.

Follow the cairned path to the trig pillar on Millstone Edge, passing the Dinner Stone, a large dining table-shaped stone set slightly apart from the edge. From the trig pillar continue along the Pennine Way, crossing three stiles, all signed with Oldham Way markers, to a fingerpost which directs you right, along a sandy track to the A62.

Those needing refreshment can bear right, down the road for 400 metres to the Floating Light public house. Two conflicting stories tell how it gained its unusual name: one states that the first landlord, a sea captain, named it after an illuminated buoy in the Mersey estuary; the other claims it was because the pub appears to be a light hanging in the sky when viewed from nearby Diggle at night. The pub is well used to walkers, providing a warm welcome to hundreds of Pennine Wayfarers every year.

If you're not tempted, cross the A62 into the car park at Brun Clough Reservoir and turn left up a flight of stone steps by the Pennine Way information board. A track beyond carries you over a stile and on to the moorland path above Redbrook Reservoir.

About 800 metres past the stile the path forks; take the stone steps on your right, on to a new flag path which leads, in another 800 metres, to Black Moss Reservoir. Bear left along the north side of the dam, along the Pennine Way, which passes between Black Moss and Swellands Reservoir, both built to provide water for the Huddersfield Narrow Canal. The Way carries you along another newly flagged section into Blakely Clough, to cross the stream by a small silt trap. Past two small waterfalls

Top: An unusual Kirklees Way marker stone near Butterley Reservoir, above Marsden.

Opposite: The steep descent into the Wessenden Valley.

you'll reach a water main cover; bearing left of this will bring you to a steep path (slippery when wet) down the clough-edge to a footbridge over the Wessenden Brook.

Turn left over the bridge, then right, up a few rough stone steps. The path climbs the embankment to a vehicle track along which you turn left down the valley, past Blakely Reservoir, beautiful in summer when the rhododendron which cloaks its banks is in flower, and Butterley Reservoir, last and lowest of the four reservoirs in the Wessenden Valley to be built; it must have caused some concern in Marsden when it started to leak on completion in 1906.

The track leads to Binn Road. Turn left for a few metres, then left through a gate and down a flight of some 211 steps into Marsden. At the bottom a dirt track to your right leads you through Bank Bottom mills back into Binn Lane.

To return to Tunnel End, turn left and cross into Fall Lane. Just before the end of Fall Lane turn left, under a road bridge, then first left, over a brook, and ahead past St Bartholomew's Church. Beyond, climb Station Road and, by the railway station at the top, turn left along the canal towpath, back to Tunnel End.

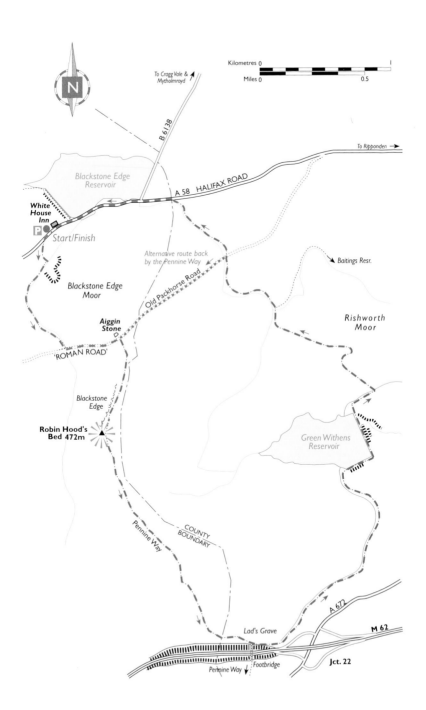

BLACKSTONE EDGE

A t Blackstone Edge you'll find the South Pennines at their narrowest. This has probably been an important crossing point since man first settled in the region and several ancient routes climb from Yorkshire into Lancashire here, the latest being the A58. The climb was made by writer Daniel Defoe, travelling in a carriage during an unseasonable blizzard in 1724. He described it as the English Andes and the journey scared the pants off him: "the depth of the precipice and the narrowness of the way looked horrid to us," he recorded. Things can't have been that bad – the White House pub at the top of the pass had been open since 1671, known then as the Coach and Horses.

Your way is more gentle, starting from the White House near the highest point of the pass. Turn left out of the car park below the pub for 50 m, then cross the A58 and follow the Pennine Way sign, up through old quarries for 50 m, to a concrete-lined water course. The firm track at the side of the channel carries you to the junction with a wide, stone-setted track which climbs to meet you.

Despite what is printed on the Ordnance Survey map, opinion as to whether this is a genuine Roman road is divided. Although it seems likely that a Roman road, between forts at Mancunium (Manchester) and Olicana (Ilkley), did cross the Pennines in this area, the flagged road is more likely to indicate a 12th century route between one landowner's two estates in Rochdale and Elland, improved for packhorse traffic in the 18th century.

Turn left up this track which rises to the re-erected Aiggin Stone, near the top, opposite a gate in the fence on

INFORMATION

Distance: 11 km (7 miles).

Start and finish: Car park on the A58, just below the White House public house, overlooking Littleborough.

Terrain: Moorland paths. Waterproofs and boots recommended, along with the Ordnance Survey map and compass.

Public transport: Buses from Halifax, Rochdale and Littleborough; alight at the White House.

Refreshments: The White House, at the start of the walk, is a popular halt for thirsty Pennine Wayfarers. An ice cream van also regularly plies for trade in a nearby layby.

'Roman' road which climbs on to Blackstone Edge.

The exposed trig pillar on Blackstone Edge.

the right. Aiggin, or agin, means 'edge' and the 2m-tall Aiggin Stone, which stood at the highest point on the old road, is an old guide stoop which might once have been a cross – an inscribed cross can still be seen on the shaft. It has been used as a boundary stone, inscribed with the date 1817 and with the letter 'S' for the district of Soyland, and also marks the Yorkshire/Lancashire boundary.

Pass through the gate opposite to follow the Pennine Way south, indicated by marker posts and cairns, to the imposing weathered gritstone outcrop along Blackstone Edge, known as Robin Hood's Bed. The views from here are as impressive as the worn stone formations that surround you, from the flat plains of Greater Manchester to the West Pennine Moors, Stoodley Pike, Boulsworth Hill and the far-off moors of the Dark Peak.

From the trig pillar on the Edge, the way soon becomes obvious thanks to the raised path created by the Pennine Way Co-ordination Project, to combat erosion caused by the tens of thousands of pairs of boots which follow the Way every year. After 1.5km the ground falls away at your feet to reveal, in dramatic fashion, the constant stream of trans-Pennine traffic on the M62 crossing the Yorkshire/Lancashire border at the road's highest point. A line of cairns leads to the footbridge across the motorway, and those of a more nervous disposition might baulk at the thought of watching the traffic from the narrow span, though that is not your way today.

Instead turn left in front of the bridge, signed for Green Withens Reservoir, for 100 m, then take the permissive path along the right hand side of the catchwater drain, which curls north to Green Withens Reservoir. When this 1400 million litre capacity dam was being built, between 1892 and 1898, a one-metre gauge railway carried stone from a quarry at neaby Booth Wood.

The path crosses the dam wall to turn right along another drain for 100 m, crossing it left on a footbridge, signed Blackstone Edge and Baitings.

Marker poles indicate the way uphill, working left under Flint Hill on Rishworth Moor before, after only a few hundred metres, running alongside a shallow drain which flows into Rishworth Drain. Ignore the sign for Baitings Reservoir and follow the drain, later signed for Blackstone Edge, straight ahead back to the A58, to turn left for 1km back to the car park.

Green Withens reservoir, looking towards Blackstone Edge.

For a more rural return from Rishworth Drain, turn left over a footbridge where you see the sign 'Pennine Way, Roman Road', and climb back to the Aiggin Stone on the sunken old packhorse route, which can be extremely wet. From the Aiggin Stone turn right on the Pennine Way, back to the White House.

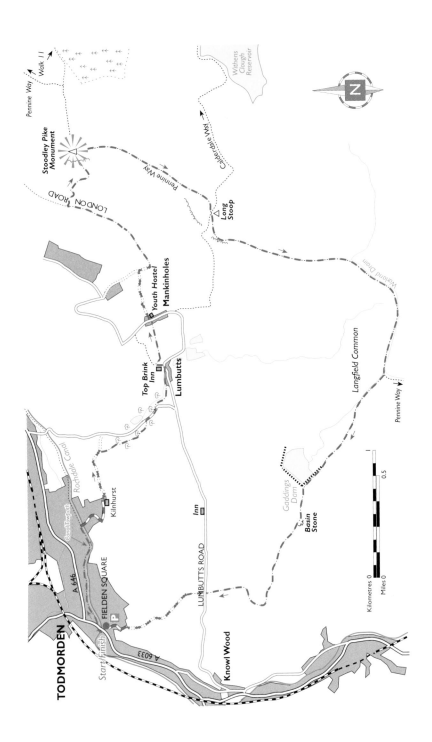

STOODLEY PIKE FROM TODMORDEN

William Holt, born in Todmorden in 1897, was one of the South Pennines' most colourful characters. The weaver became a familiar figure across the nation for his BBC broadcasts and his travels on horseback, during which he would sell his self-published books door-to-door. This splendid route passes two sites with Holt associations as well as visiting Stoodley Pike.

Join the Rochdale Canal towpath at Todmorden Lock, by the library in Rochdale Road, and pass under the road bridge. At the second bridge beyond the lock, cross the canal to climb Kilnhurst Road. At the end of the road, in front of two garages, turn right.

INFORMATION

Distance: 14 km (9 miles).

Start and finish: Fielden Square in Rochdale Road, Todmorden. There is a small car park in front of the Golden Lion pub in the square.

Terrain: From wooded cloughs to open moor. Boots and waterproofs recommended.

Public transport: Buses and trains from Burnley, Halifax and Rochdale pass through Todmorden.

Refreshments: Pubs, restaurants and cafes in Todmorden. The walk passes the Top Brink pub in Lumbutts.

Leisure craft on the restored Rochdale Canal, Todmorden.

Kilnhurst, the splendid house on the right was, between 1933 and 1973, home to William Holt. Son of a coal merchant, Holt left his job as a weaver in 1914 , aged 16, to fight with the Lancashire Fusiliers. He returned to open a holiday camp at Hardcastle Crags, then travelled the world working as an English teacher in Spain, a logger and weaver in Canada and film stuntman in Berlin.

It was at Kilnhurst that he wrote the books for which he is best remembered, including *I Haven't Unpacked*, *The Weaver's Knot* and *The Wizard of Whirlaw*. Holt became a regular broadcaster on the BBC, and he and his horse Trigger became familiar figures throughout the north of England. He died in 1977; Trigger, who outlived him by three years, is buried in a field nearby.

Enter the delightful walled lane left of the house, which carries you through Oldroyd for 100m, where you turn right past three wooden garages. Climb the stile to follow a field path to another stile, beyond which an obvious line leads you through Causeway Wood, eventually descending gently to Causeway Wood Road.

Head up the road for 100m and take the signed path left, down into the clough bottom. The path soon rises on a grassy track to enter Lumbutts. Turn left, past Lumbutts Mill Activity Centre, a former textile mill.

Over the bridge in front of the mill, bear left up the Calderdale Way, to the Top Brink Inn. A stile right of the pub puts you on a short flagged path to Mankinholes.

The view of Stoodley Pike from the Pennine Way.

Cross the road and follow the bridleway, past the Youth Hostel entrance, for 400m. At the end turn right for 100m, then left, along London Road for slightly more than a kilometre. By a stile on the left, a steep path leads right, up the moor to Stoodley Pike (the monument is described in Walk 11).

From the monument head south along the cairned Pennine Way, which crosses the Calderdale Way at a large stone pillar, known as Long Stoop. Your way lies straight ahead but 300m to the left, along the Calderdale Way, the Te Deum stone is worth a brief detour. The stone, inscribed Te Deum Laudamus (We Praise Thee O Lord), was a resting spot used by bearers carrying coffins from Cragg Vale for burial at Mankinholes.

Back on the Pennine Way, 2km beyond Long Stoop, you reach a sluice gate on Warland Drain. A Todmorden Centenary Way link path marker on the right guides you across the moor, to Gaddings Dam.

Pick your way to the left edge of the dam and walk along the embankment; a waymarker at the end puts you on an obvious path which, in 300m, reaches the Basin Stone, used for Chartist meetings in the 1830s and in 1926 by William Holt, who wanted to found a new religion "of physical action against evil, of utter self-

The Basin Stone, where William Holt attempted to found a new religion.

denial". Holt's concern for social matters led him into politics: he represented the Communist Party on the local council but was scolded for writing about the laughter of millgirls holidaying in Blackpool – Party members felt this presented victims of capitalism in too happy a light!

The path actually veers right just before the Basin Stone, at a point indicated by another Centenary Way link path marker. A kilometre along the faint path you cross the old Rake Gate packhorse route to curve right, downhill to a black gate in the intake wall. The path beyond heads, round the house at the bottom, down to Lumbutts Road. Through the wicket gate opposite a field path leads to a gap stile on the right, which puts you on dusty Shoebroad Lane. Turn left down the lane, which carries you down, past the Unitarian Church, to Fielden Square in Todmorden.

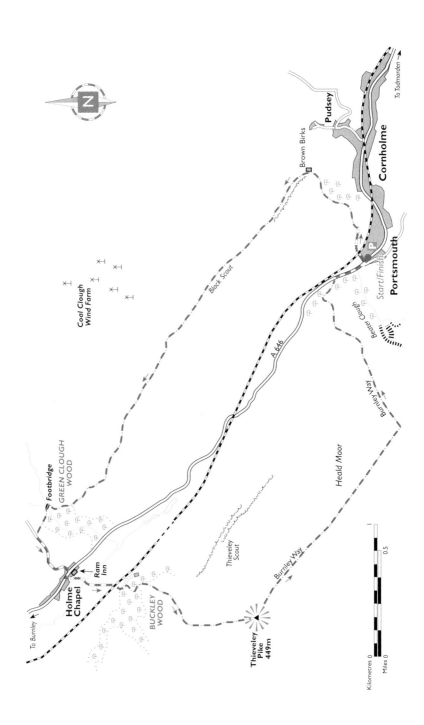

Pudsey

Brown Birks

Cornholme

To Todmorden

Block Scout

Coal Clough
Wind Farm

Start/Finish

Portsmouth

Bearer Clough

A 646

Burnley Way

Heald Moor

Footbridge

GREEN CLOUGH
WOOD

Thieveley
Scout

Burnley Way

Ram
Inn

To Burnley

Holme
Chapel

BUCKLEY
WOOD

Thieveley
Pike
449m

Kilometres 0

Miles 0

0.5

1

THE CLIVIGER GORGE

The Cliviger Gorge arouses as much excitement among geologists as it does among walkers. The valley, which gives birth to not one but two River Calders – one each for Yorkshire and Lancashire – contains some of the best evidence of the Ice Age to be found. A fault in the rock stratas enabled a huge river of meltwater pouring from the retreating ice sheets to carve a valley within a valley, leaving moorland cloughs hanging high above the main valley floor and exposing bands of sandstone and shale. Coal and lead ore have both been extracted in the area.

For the walker, however, the area offers rich upland walking with fine views of the South Pennines, the Yorkshire Dales, the West Pennine Moors and Pendle and the Forest of Bowland.

The view across Portsmouth.

From Portsmouth head up Station Parade, which is 100m down Burnley Road from the Roebuck Inn. Cross the railway line with care and climb the track ahead. Before Monks Royd House bear right over a stile to a Burnley Way marker post, to turn uphill on an obvious waymarked path. Where the path forks, bear left up to Brown Birks Farm.

Turn left by the farmhouse, up a track which carries you on to the moor. You soon pass through a field gate, then bear slightly left to a marker post

INFORMATION

Distance: 13 km (8 miles).

Start and finish: Portsmouth, on the A646 Burnley Road near Todmorden. There is a car park 100m from the Roebuck Inn in Burnley Road.

Terrain: A relatively high-level walk, with sections of open moor. Conditions are reasonable underfoot but could deteriorate after a period of bad weather. There are two noticeable ascents, from 190m above sea level to a maximum of 449m. Boots and waterproofs advisable.

Public transport: Portsmouth is served by buses from Halifax, Hebden Bridge, Todmorden, Burnley, Littleborough and Rochdale. The walk could be cut short by catching a Todmorden-bound bus from Holme Chapel, halfway round.

Refreshments: Pubs in Portsmouth and Holme Chapel, at the halfway stage.

Note: Opencast workings shown below Thieveley Pike on the OS South Pennines map are no longer visible.

to follow the wallside. Gaps in the wall give you excellent views of the sandstone buttresses, formed by streams cutting through the glacier-exposed rock bands on the opposite side of the valley.

Pendle Hill, with its strong associations with witchcraft, is in full view by the time you reach the small building which controls the power output from the wind turbines; cross the wall here by a stile on your left and continue down the other side to the end of the wall. There a line of reeds guides your way across a field to a wooden step stile. Cross that and pass through a broken wall on your right to follow the clough down, on the opposite bank, the initially indistinct path soon becoming a grassy track. Bear right on the track met at the bottom, past the restored house and barn at Light Birks, and over a stile beyond.

The Ram Inn, Holme Chapel.

Follow the wall ahead along the top of Green Clough Wood, winding down to cross a footbridge across the clough. Over a stile bear left, to a waymarker and, beyond, a wooden step stile. Climb, with the wall on your left, to another stile, over which a gravel path carries you down to a surfaced lane which drops into Holme Chapel, opposite the Ram Inn. The village takes its name from a private chantry chapel built by Richard Whitaker in 1533.

The Ram Inn is believed to be the oldest in the Cliviger valley and gained its name in the 19th century, to commemorate local farmers' involvement in creating the East Lancashire Lonk, a hardy breed of sheep.

Take the signed path behind the bus stop, right of the Ram; it carries you under the railway and a small, ornate bridge, which carried a private path from the Whitakers' home to the village railway station. Turn right in front of a cattle grid, up a fenced path through Buckley Wood, on the Burnley Way.

At the top a step stile delivers you on to moorland pasture, where the waymarked Burnley Way leads up through farm ruins and over a step stile by a wooden gate to follow an obvious green track uphill. This soon fades to a cairned path, crossing a harder track to climb to the summit trig pillar.

The view is superb. Ahead, Bacup sits beneath Cowpe Moor, to the left of which are Winter Hill, Rivington and Darwen's Jubilee Tower. Right of Hameldon Hill's masts is distinctive Pendle, the Forest of Bowland's fells peering over its shoulder on one side and the Yorkshire Dales, behind Burnley, on the other.

From the trig pillar cross the wall by a stile 15m away to turn left on a path which veers gently away from the wall, crossing the moor to a wooden stile. The grassy path beyond sticks to the left of the wall for 350m, to a small cairn where you leave the wall to follow the wide crest of Heald Moor.

A kilometre of fine walking beyond that cairn you reach a discreet wooden marker post, pointing left. The path is hard to make out but, should you lose it, head for Cornholme's mill chimneys until you reach

Among the turbines at Coal Clough wind power station.

a wall. There, look for a stile and marker pole, left of an old shed on the other side of the wall. Climb the stile and drop 20m to head left, down a rough track which winds past a ruined farm and, through fields, brings you back to Portsmouth, near the Roe Buck Inn.

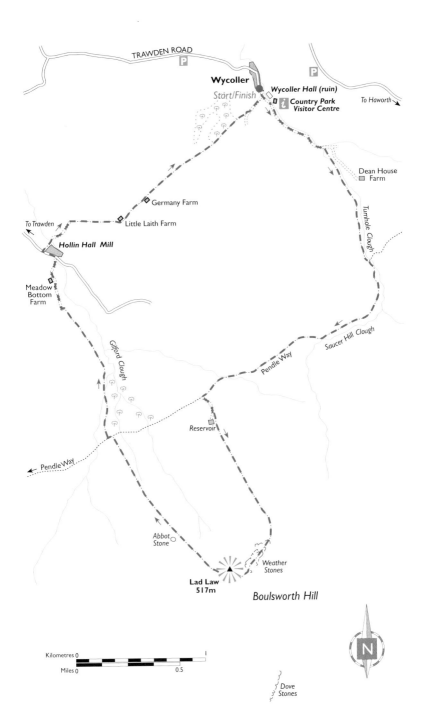

TRAWDEN ROAD

P

Wycoller
Start/Finish

Wycoller Hall (ruin)

P

To Haworth

Country Park
Visitor Centre

Dean House
Farm

Germany Farm

Little Laith Farm

To Trawden

Hollin Hall Mill

Turnhole Clough

Meadow
Bottom
Farm

Gilford Clough

Saucer Hill Clough

Pendle Way

Reservoir

Pendle Way

Abbot
Stone

Weather
Stones

**Lad Law
517m**

Boulsworth Hill

Kilometres 0   1

Miles 0   0.5

N

Dove
Stones

LAD LAW AND WYCOLLER

Boulsworth Hill is, at 517m (1,696 ft), the highest point in the South Pennines. The view from its summit is more than ample reward for the stiff climb: on a clear day you can pick out Blackpool Tower and Southport sands on the west coast, the high tops of the Yorkshire Dales, while Pendle Hill and the Forest of Bowland are spread at your feet.

The moors are part of the South Pennines Special Protection Area, designated under European law, because of their importance for ground nesting moorland birds. The heather-clad southern slopes and the grassy northern flanks provide a varied habitat and you stand every chance of seeing peregrine, golden plover and snipe, while buzzard and harriers are more occasional visitors.

The ruins of Wycoller Hall, model for Ferndean Manor in Charlotte Brontë's *Jane Eyre*.

Once a thriving community of farmers and weavers, Wycoller is now a beautiful hamlet almost untouched by the 20th century. The Industrial Revolution saw production and employment migrate to large mill towns; Wycoller was emptied by the water authorities to make way for a new reservoir.

The scheme was never carried out and since the 1940s much of the area has been turned into a

INFORMATION

Distance: 13 km (8 miles).

Start and finish: Wycoller village. Cars should be left at either Trawden Road car park, off the B6250, or the Haworth Road car park, off the Colne/Haworth road. From the former a surfaced lane is followed into the village and from the latter well-signed field paths drop steeply into the dean.

Terrain: This walk goes from wooded clough to wild open moor and back. Boots and waterproofs are recommended.

Public transport: There are no bus services to Wycoller; services from Keighley, Nelson and Colne stop at Laneshaw Bridge,.

Refreshments: None on route; but the small cafe in Wycoller.

Opening hours: The aisled barn is open at weekends, 0900-1700. Contact 01282 863627.

Note: The path to Boulsworth Hill summit is a concessionary route provided by North West Water.

country park, with its important aisled barn converted into a small museum-cum-information centre.

From the barn, cross the beck and head upstream along the track. You soon reach a junction, by the tracks for Dean House Farm and Parson Lee Farm. Cross the stile on your right to follow the streamside path up Turnhole Clough, over one footbridge and then upstream towards a second. Cross the stile in front of the bridge, staying on this bank.

The path rises to the top of the wood and crosses a stile to follow a fence. Marker poles help when the way seems vague. Drop to the water's edge then climb a stile – a few stone steps to the right keep you on the path which again climbs above the stream to a stile, over which you join a rough track past an old boundary stone. From here the walk takes on a wilder moorland aspect – a packhorse track guides the way sporadically, as do Pendle Way markers.

The path runs alongside Saucer Hill Clough, on the left, to a junction with a surfaced lane. A few metres further on the yellow-posted concessionary path up Boulsworth Hill climbs left, up the hillside, from the service track of a small reservoir building. As you meet the crest of the hill bear right, past the curious Weather Stones, to Boulsworth's summit, Lad Law, a name thought to be derived from the Celtic Llad, meaning slaughter and Law, meaning hill; some think an altar-like stone near the trig

On Lad Law, summit of
Boulsworth Hill.

pillar was used by druids for sacrificial offerings.

The moors around Boulsworth are some of the wildest and most impressive in the entire Pennine chain. Dramatic stone outcrops, such as Dovestones to the south, are visible nearby and in summer the plateau is swathed in the bobbing white heads of hare's tail cotton grass. Much of the area is out of bounds but a vigorous campaign for access is being fought locally.

From the trig pillar a further line of posts to the left, looking north, indicates the way back down past the mitre-shaped Abbot Stone and, over a stile and two muddy streams, to the lane.

Here you turn left for 20 m to a field gate, into Gilford Clough. Walk parallel to the stream on a barely visible old track. Don't be tempted down the bank by one of several sheep tracks – the track itself drops to a footbridge after a few more metres. Beyond this, cross a stile and follow the fingerposted path up the field, keeping left of a septic tank in front of a farm. Turn left at the gable end of the building ahead, then right on to the track past Tongue End Farm.

The track carries you past Meadow Bottom Farm then right, down to Hollin Hall Mill. Turn left, past the mill, then right over a bridge and up the track ahead to a path junction. Go right, through a wooden gate (not the stone gap stile).

Following the field edge to Little Laith Farm, climb the stone stile in the field corner. The hedged path beyond leads to the farmyard: pass through the second of two gates on your right, then turn left down the field edge – marker posts show the way.

Beyond the next two stiles walk around the left side of Germany Farm, to join the track beyond. The route leads straight as a die from here, over a variety of stiles, into a young plantation at the foot of which you go through a gate, down to the track, and turn left back into Wycoller.

INDEX

Other titles in this series

25 Walks – In and Around Aberdeen
25 Walks – Arrochar, Cowal and Bute
25 Walks – In and Around Belfast
25 Walks – The Chilterns
25 Walks – The Cotswolds
25 Walks – Deeside
25 Walks – Dumfries and Galloway
25 Walks – Edinburgh and Lothian
25 Walks – Fife
25 Walks – In and Around Glasgow
25 Walks – In and Around London
25 Walks – Highland Perthshire
25 Walks – The Scottish Borders
25 Walks – The Trossachs
25 Walks – The Western Isles
25 Walks – The Yorkshire Dales

Glencoe and Lochaber Hill Walks
Simple Map Reading

Forthcoming

The Cairngorms Hill Walks
An Introduction to Walking

Long distance guides published by The Stationery Office

The West Highland Way – Official Guide
The Southern Upland Way – Official Guide
St Cuthbert's Way – Official Guide

The **Stationery Office**

Published by The Stationery Office and available from:

The Stationery Office Bookshops
71 Lothian Road, Edinburgh EH3 9AZ
(counter service only)
59-60 Holborn Viaduct, London EC1A 2FD
(Temporary location until mid-1998)
Fax 0171-831 1326
68-69 Bull Street, Birmingham B4 6AD
0121-236 9696 Fax 0121-236 9699
33 Wine Street, Bristol BS1 2BQ
0117-926 4306 Fax 0117-929 4515
9-21 Princess Street, Manchester M60 8AS
0161-834 7201 Fax 0161-833 0634
16 Arthur Street, Belfast BT1 4GD
01232 238451 Fax 01232 235401
The Stationery Office Oriel Bookshop
The Friary, Cardiff CF1 4AA
01222 395548 Fax 01222 384347

The Stationery Office publications are also available from:

The Publications Centre
(mail, telephone and fax orders only)
PO Box 276, London SW8 5DT
General enquiries 0171-873 0011
Telephone orders 0171-873 9090
Fax orders 0171-873 8200

Accredited Agents
(see Yellow Pages)

and through good booksellers